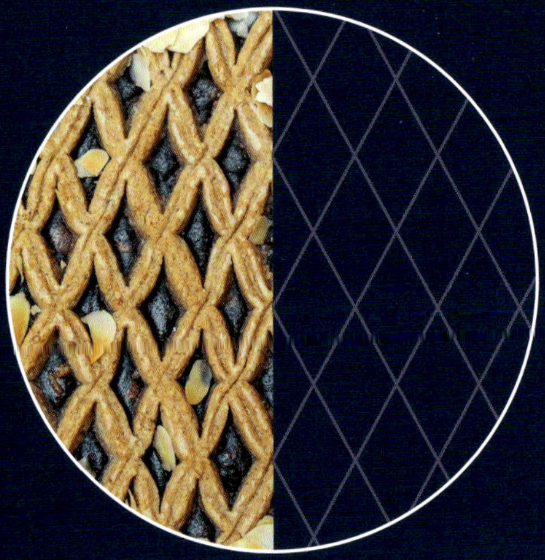

Praktische Überlegungen, wie sie diese Stadt seit jeher leiten, führten zum charakteristischen Rautenmuster der Linzer Torte: So konnte der Teig nicht reißen. Dass diese strenge und doch federleichte Geometrie entfernt an die Oberfläche elektronischer Leiterplatten erinnert, mag kein Zufall sein. Und Grund genug, „die Raute" als erstes Bild eines Bildbandes über Linz zu wählen.

Practical considerations, that have always taken precedence in this city, led to the characteristic lattice pattern of Linzer torte: It prevented the pastry from tearing. Perhaps it is no coincidence that this geometry, rigid yet light as a feather, is faintly reminiscent of the surface of electronic circuit boards. It certainly justifies the choice of "the lattice" as the first image in this illustrated book about Linz.

Fairness gehört zum Wesenskern der Linzerinnen und Linzer. Effizienz ebenso. Die männlichen Wortformen in den Texten sind deshalb ausschließlich aus Gründen der leichteren Lesbarkeit gewählt. Sie schließen Leserinnen und Leser gleichermaßen ein.

Medieninhaber: LW Werbe- und Verlags GmbH, www.lwmedia.at
Herausgeber: Erwin Goldfuss
Geschäfts- und Projektleitung: Mag. (FH) Claudia Altrichter
Text: Mag. Andreas Spannring
Fotos: Manuel Tauber-Romieri
Key Account: Claudia Altrichter, Pepi Lehner
Grafische Produktion: LWmedia, Michael Wolf
Korrektur: LWmedia, Dr. Antonia Barboric
Übersetzung: Wordworks, Neil Perkins
Trotz sorgfältiger Recherche des Autors sind Irrtümer und Änderungen vorbehalten.

ISBN 978-3-9504718-3-0

Media proprietor: LW Werbe- und Verlags GmbH, www.lwmedia.at, Austria
Publisher: Erwin Goldfuss
Project manager: Claudia Altrichter
Text: Andreas Spannring
Photos: Manuel Tauber-Romieri
Key account managers: Claudia Altrichter, Pepi Lehner
Graphic production: LWmedia, Michael Wolf
Proofreading: LWmedia, Antonia Barboric
Translation: Wordworks, Neil Perkins
Although every effort has been made to ensure the accuracy of the information contained in this book, it remains subject to errors and alteration.

ISBN 978-3-9504718-3-0

LINZ

ANDREAS SPANNRING
MANUEL TAUBER-ROMIERI

ANDREAS SPANNRING (*1963) hat seine Wurzeln im ober-
österreichischen Alpenvorland. Er arbeitet in Wien und St. Pölten als Texter und Publizist. Mit dem Stiftsgymnasium Kremsmünster hat er seine Jugend an einem Ort verbracht, der mit Linz auf vielfältige Weise verbunden ist.

ANDREAS SPANNRING (b. 1963) has his roots in the Alpine foothills in Upper Austria. He works in Vienna and Sankt Pölten as a copywriter and publicist. As an adolescent he attended the Stiftsgymnasium Kremsmünster, an institution with many links to Linz.

MANUEL TAUBER-ROMIERI (*1987) hat als gelernter Siebdrucker seinen Sinn für Strukturen und Perspektiven entwickelt. Seit 2010 arbeitet er auf selbstständiger Basis als Fotograf für in- und ausländische Auftraggeber, darunter renommierte Magazine und Buchprojekte.

MANUEL TAUBER-ROMIERI (b. 1987) developed his feeling for structures and perspectives during his training as a screen printer. Since 2010 he has worked as a freelance photographer for clients in Austria and elsewhere on projects including well-known magazines and books.

LWMEDIA ist als Agentur und Verlag spezialisiert auf hochwertige Inhalte und crossmediale Kommunikation. Zum Programm zählen führende Titel auf dem österreichischen Magazinmarkt wie „Vinaria – Magazin für Weinkultur" oder „Land der Berge". Zeitgemäß gestaltete Bildbände erscheinen für Linz, St. Pölten und Krems an der Donau.

LWMEDIA is an agency and publisher specialising in high-quality content and cross-media communication. Its portfolio includes leading Austrian magazines such as Vinaria – Magazin für Weinkultur *and* Land der Berge. *Illustrated books in a contemporary design are available for Linz, Sankt Pölten and Krems an der Donau.*

LIFE

DRIVE

VIBES

DAS LEBENDIGE ERWÄCHST AUS DEN KONTRASTE

IT IS FROM CONTRASTS THAT VITALITY IS BORN.

DIE NEUE HOFSTÆTTER APOTHEKE
dean&david

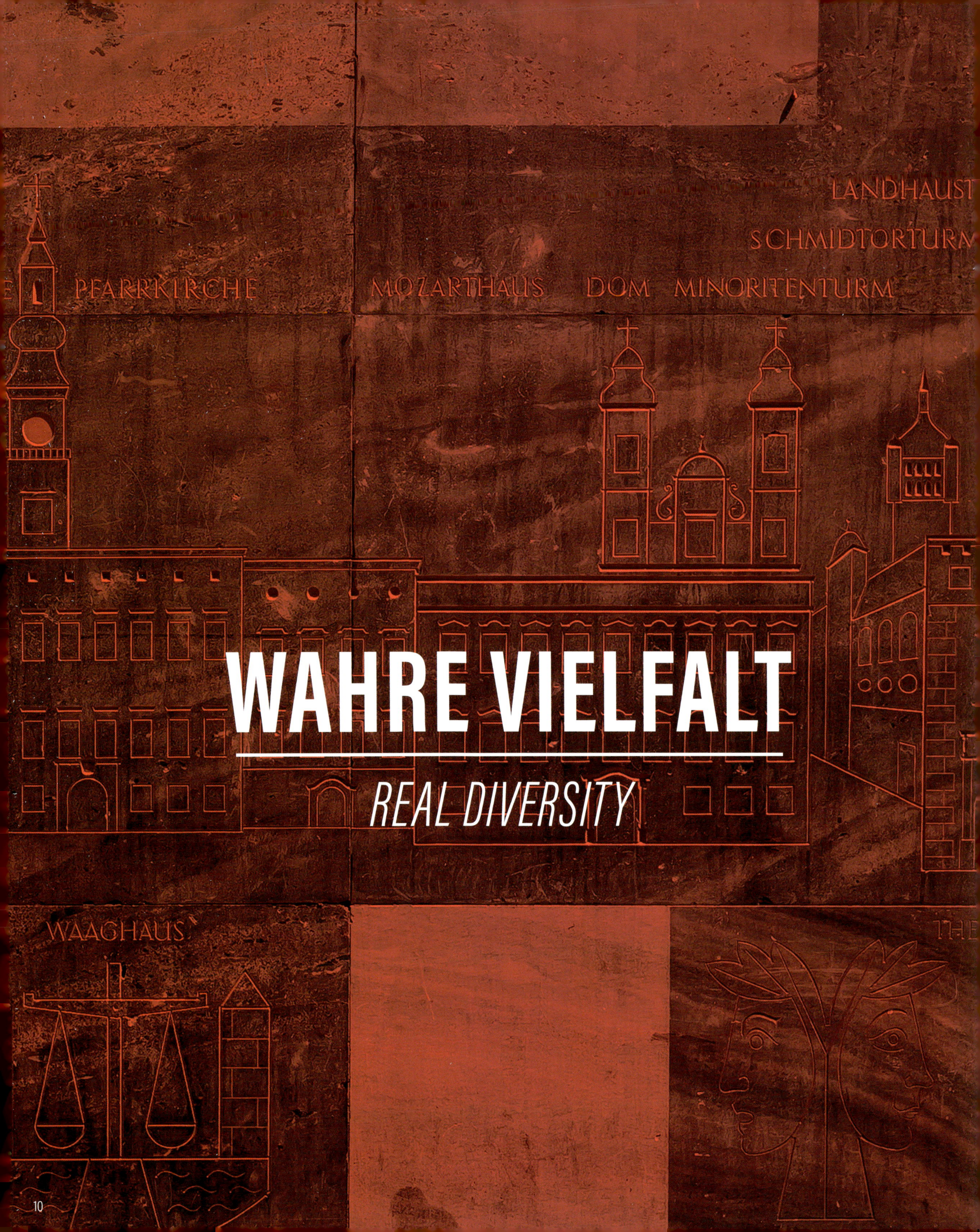

WAHRE VIELFALT

REAL DIVERSITY

1.1

Samstagvormittag auf dem Südbahnhofmarkt: Obst und Gemüse, Saftiges und Deftiges, so weit das Auge reicht. Radio Oberösterreich überträgt live ein Schaukochen. Die Stimmung liegt irgendwo zwischen oberösterreichischer Gemütlichkeit und weltläufiger Geschäftigkeit. Durch und durch Linz eben.

Saturday morning at the Südbahnhofmarkt: a panoply of fruit and veg, of the succulent and the substantial. Radio Oberösterreich is broadcasting a cooking demonstration live. The mood is somewhere between Upper Austrian conviviality and cosmopolitan bustle. In other words, Linz as it lives and breathes.

LINZER ATHLETIK - SPORTKLUB
LASK
gegr. 1908

Paradeiser, Spitzkraut und Äpfel aus der Region lassen ihn erahnen, den natürlichen Reichtum des Linzer Umlandes. Avocados, Melonen und Kumquats die Weltoffenheit. Beides nährt die Vitalität der nicht nur kulinarisch multikulturellen Stadt. Am großen Gemüsestand nahe der Lustenauer Straße gustieren soignierte Innenstadtbewohner neben Kundschaft, die mit geräumigen Taschen zu Werke geht. Per Straßenbahn ist man aus den Linzer Wohngürteln wie Kleinmünchen, Spallerhof oder dem Bindermichl angereist. Öffentliche Frei- und Grünräume haben dort Vorrang vor eigenbrötlerischem „Gartln", wo Industrie und Genossenschaften seit Generationen großvolumig Wohnraum geschaffen haben.

Zwischen Kaffeerösterei, Shiitake-Pilzen und Bio-Bachsaiblingen mischt sich, geschmackvoll in Casual Wear, die „Generation Executive" unters Volk. Geschäftliche Assets zählen ebenso wie Regionalität und Saisonalität zum Kanon der Werte. Mit der bevorzugten Wohngegend – gerne dort, wo sich die Übersicht gut wahren lässt: in den stylishen Hochbauten des modernen Linz. In den Höhenlagen Urfahrs oder auf dem Römerberg, wo die nahen Türme, Häuser und Schlote der Stadt vor tuckernden Traktoren auf dem Feld wie eine surreale Tapete wirken.

Die pensionierten Industriearbeiter im Schanigarten der „Mosteria" pflegen ihre eigene Art der Übersicht. Morgen spielt der Linzer Traditionsverein LASK im Fußballcup. „Des pack ma!", sagt der, der die Karten mischt. Nicken in der Runde. Durch und durch Linz.

Tomatoes, cabbage and apples from the region hint at the abundance provided by nature in the area around Linz. Avocados, melons and kumquats at a global perspective. Both fuel the vitality of a city whose multicultural character is not limited to food alone. At the big vegetable stall near Lustenauer Strasse, well-dressed city-centre residents browse and sample alongside customers with capacious bags. The latter have come in by tram from residential belts such as Kleinmünchen, Spallerhof and Bindermichl where public green spaces take priority over solitary recreational gardening, and where industry and cooperatives have been creating expansive residential areas for generations.

Between coffee roasting stalls, shiitake and organic brook trout the "executive generation", tastefully dressed in casual wear, mingles with the populace. The values upheld here include business assets as well as local and seasonal produce. The favoured neighbourhood: where it is easy to see further. In the stylish high-rises of modern Linz. In the hills of Urfahr or on the Römerberg where the nearby towers, houses and chimneys of the city, with tractors chugging on the fields behind, appear like surreal wallpaper.

The retired factory workers in the beer garden of the "Mosteria" have their own views. Tomorrow LASK, the football club with the greatest tradition in Linz, has a cup game. "We'll win that!" says the one shuffling the cards. The others nod. Linz as it lives and breathes.

ALTE STADT, JUNGER SPIRIT

OLD TOWN, YOUNG SPIRIT

Pittoresk verwinkelt atmet die Altstadt rund um das Kremsmünsterer Stiftshaus spätmittelalterlichen Charme. Zwischen Renaissance und Barock, Erkern und Höfen haben sich Bars, Pubs und Galerien gemütlich eingerichtet. Vor allcm zu vorgerückter Stunde lassen Nachtschwärmer den alten Kern der Stadt ziemlich jung aussehen.

The picturesque and labyrinthine lanes of the old quarter around the Kremsmünsterer Haus exude late-medieval charm. Bars, pubs and art galleries have found cosy homes amid the Renaissance and the Baroque, the oriels and courtyards. And in the small hours, late-night revellers make the city's old heart seem young again.

LICHTGESTALT
SHINING LIGHT

Immer steiler den Schlossberg hinan führt vom Hauptplatz weg die Hofgasse. Auf dem Platz beim Hofberg setzt der 2018 errichtete „Lichtbrunnen" moderne Akzente. Eine Reminiszenz an den einstigen „Wasserbrunnen", der hier den historischen Marktplatz der Linzer Altstadt schmückte.

From the main square, Hofgasse leads up to the castle hill, rising ever more steeply. The "light fountain", erected in 2018, lends the square by Hofberg a modern touch. It harks back to the water fountain that once adorned the historic market square in Linz old town.

VEGAN
rivelles

WOHNKRAFT

HOME ADVANTAGE

Sozialer Wohnbau machte Linz so bevölkerungsstark, wie es die Wirtschaftsstärke der Stadt erforderte. Beginnend mit dem Werkssiedlungsbau der Verstaatlichten bis zu den komfortablen Genossenschaftswohnungen der Gegenwart.

Public housing brought people to Linz in the numbers required by the city's booming economy. It began with accommodation for workers in nationalised industry and today takes the form of comfortable cooperative flats.

SONNENPLATZ

A PLACE IN THE SUN

Die Solar City im Stadtteil Pichling bietet 1.300 ökologisch konzipierte Wohnungen und unverwechselbares Lebensgefühl. Realisiert und 2005 eröffnet wurde die Solar City nach den Plänen von Architektur-Weltstar Norman Foster.

Solar City in the Pichling district has 1,300 homes designed on ecological principles and offering a lifestyle all its own. Solar City was built according to plans by star architect Norman Foster and opened in 2005.

SPAR

ÜBERSICHT

OVERVIEW

Mehr Höhe beim Bauen lässt mehr (Grün)Raum auf dem Boden. Der Lux Tower nahe dem Hauptbahnhof war eigentlich als Büroturm geplant. Heute leben in ihm auch viele, die es beim Wohnen gern übersichtlich haben.

The taller the building, the more (green) space there is on the ground. Lux Tower near Linz central station was originally conceived as an office complex. Today it is the home of many people who like to take a broader view of things.

XXXL RABATTE
75 JAHRE
75 JAHRE

HIER DAHEIM, ÜBERALL ZU HAUSE

ROOTS AND BRANCHES

Wohnkomfort war und bleibt in der wirtschaftlichen Boomstadt Linz ein Dauerbrenner. Mit ihren oberösterreichischen Wurzeln angemessen vor Ort repräsentiert ist die XXXLutz-Gruppe, heute eines der größten Möbelhäuser weltweit. Nicht zuletzt die hauseigene Marke Mömax übersetzt das traditionelle Linzer Wohnmotto auf moderne Ansprüche: „Praktisch, modern, preiswert!"

Home comforts have always been in great demand in Linz, an economic and industrial boom town. The XXXLutz Group, one of the world's biggest furniture stores, has its roots in Upper Austria, and this is reflected in its presence in the region. The group's own Mömax brand also plays a major role in bringing the traditional Linz motto for furnishings and interiors in line with today's requirements: "Practical, modern, good value!"

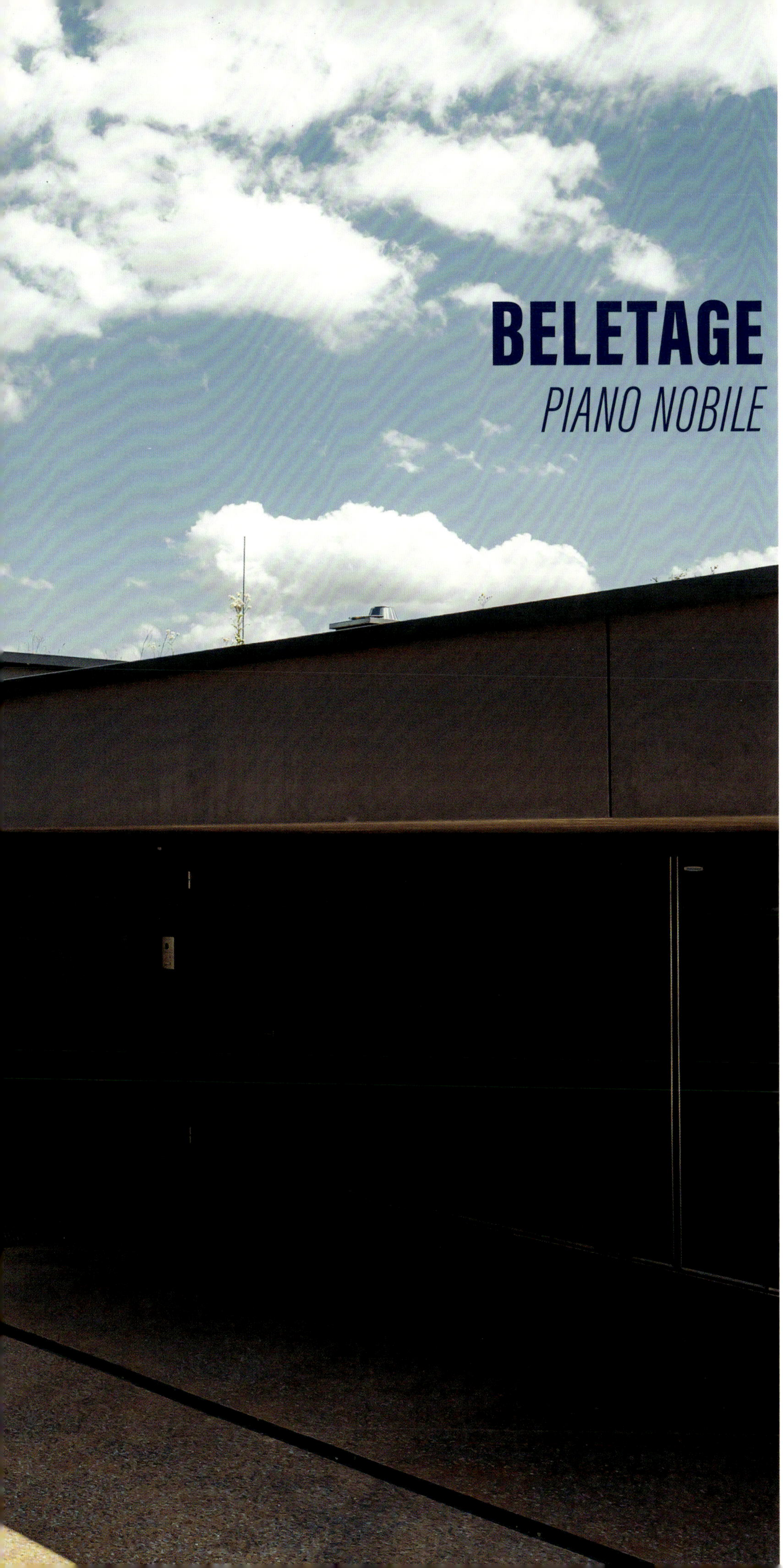

BELETAGE

PIANO NOBILE

Urban-ländlich hebt sich die Szenerie direkt von der Linzer Innenstadt zur krönenden Basilika auf dem Pöstlingberg. Eine Qualität, die hier stilvolle Villen ebenso wachsen lässt wie die Bodenpreise.

The landscape rises from Linz city centre in an urban-rural melange up to the basilica that crowns the Pöstlingberg. A circumstance that results in elegant villas and top property prices.

ZEICHEN AUF ZEICHEN

STATUE STATEMENTS

Metall ist den Linzern vertraut. Dementsprechend gerne nutzen sie den Donaupark mit seinen stählernen Skulpturen als Treffpunkt, zur Mittagspause oder einfach um ihre Zeichen auf den Zeichen zu hinterlassen.

Metal is something the people of Linz have an affinity with. That is why they like to meet at the Donaupark with its steel sculptures, at lunchtime or simply to leave their mark on these landmarks.

FLANIERMEILE

PROMENADE

1,3 Kilometer misst das längste Einkaufsvergnügen von Linz entlang der Landstraße. Fußgänger haben hier Vorrang. Dicht an dicht reihen sich opulente Einkaufsmärkte und Restaurants an Geschäfte, die schon morgen als „Geheimtipp" gehandelt werden.

The longest shopping El Dorado in Linz stretches for 1.3 km along Landstrasse. Here, pedestrians have priority. Luxurious emporiums and restaurants stand cheek by jowl with shops that will be tomorrow's insiders' tips.

Marc O'Polo
ROLEX
APOTHEKE

LINZER SHOPPING-IKONE

LINZ SHOPPING TEMPLE

Zum Urknall des Konsumzeitalters geriet 1963 die Eröffnung des Passage Kaufhaus an der Landstraße. Erlebnishungrige kamen von nah und fern, um die Fahrt auf einer der ersten Rolltreppen in Oberösterreich zu wagen. Heute ist es eher die Shopping-Vielfalt auf sieben Etagen, die dem Haus einen Platz unter den am stärksten frequentierten innerstädtischen Einkaufszentren Österreichs sichert.

The big bang of the consumer era was the opening of the Passage department store on Landstrasse in 1963. Novelty-seekers came from near and far to test their nerve on one of the first escalators in Upper Austria. Today it is more the diversity of shops on seven floors that makes the building one of the most popular inner-city shopping malls in Austria.

SAISONAL

CHANGING WITH THE SEASONS

Das Epizentrum des Genusses finden Anspruchsvolle auf dem Südbahnhofmarkt. Von saisonalem Obst und Gemüse über regionale Fleisch- und Fischspezialitäten: An 28 fixen Marktständen bietet der größte Grünmarkt Österreichs alles, wonach Herz und Gaumen verlangen.

The epicentre for epicureans is the Südbahnhofmarkt. On 28 permanent market stalls, Austria's biggest food market has everything the heart, and palate, desires: from seasonal fruit and vegetables to local meat and fish specialities.

DER KAFFEE IST FERTIG

COFFEE'S READY!

Kaffeehaus-Charme der altösterreichischen Art hat auch im pragmatischen Linz seinen Platz und seine Liebhaber. Seit 1847 steht „das Traxlmayr“ für Kaffeekultur nach Wiener Vorbild und nach Linzer Art.

Coffee shop charm in the traditional Austrian style has its place and its aficionados even in pragmatic Linz. Since 1847 the Traxlmayr has stood for coffee shop culture inspired by Vienna but with its own local flavour.

TRADITIONELL MODERN

TRADITIONALLY MODERN

In der „Startrampe" der Sparkasse OÖ entwickeln Jungunternehmer ihre Geschäftsideen – mit der Sparkasse OÖ als starkem Bankpartner an ihrer Seite. Was sich im Look & Feel der Zentrale in der Linzer Promenade ausdrückt, verkörpert zugleich die Philosophie der Regionalbank: die Verbindung von Tradition mit der Moderne. Neben dem „Banking der Zukunft" findet sie ihren Ausdruck in vielfältigem Engagement in den Regionen: von der Bildung über die Kultur bis zum Sport.

At the "Startrampe" (launch pad) run by the Sparkasse Upper Austria bank, young entrepreneurs develop their business ideas – with the bank as a strong partner. The look and feel of the regional bank's headquarters on Promenade in Linz embodies its philosophy: connecting tradition with modernity. This is expressed not just in "banking of the future", but also in the bank's involvement in a wide range of activities in the surrounding area: from education to culture to sport.

Leberkas-Pepi

HERZHAFT

HEARTY

Schlankmacher sind die würzigen Spezialitäten beim Leberkas-Pepi nur bei diszipliniertem Genuss. Glücklichmacher sind sie allemal. Die Palette reicht vom klassischen Leberkäsbrät bis zum „Teuferl", das den Chili in sich hat.

The spicy specialities served at Leberkas-Pepi are only likely to help slimmers when enjoyed in moderation. But while they may not make customers slim, they certainly make them happy. The options range from classic fried leberkäse to the "Teuferl" with a chilli kick.

SOMMERSPLASH MIT KLASSE

SUMMER SPLASH WITH STYLE

Seit bald 100 Jahren versammelt das Parkbad in bester Innenstadtlage nächst dem Brucknerhaus Wasserratten und Sonnenanbeter. Schon die gediegene Fassade aus den späten 1930er-Jahren verrät es: Hier ist Baden eine Frage des Stils!

The Parkbad next to the Brucknerhaus in a prime central location has attracted water lovers and sun worshippers for nearly 100 years. The tasteful late-1930s facade is enough to show that this is a pool with class!

VOLKES GARTEN

THE PEOPLE'S GARDEN

Mit mürrischer Würde blickt Franz Stelzhamer (1802–1874), Dichter der oberösterreichischen Landeshymne, in den Volksgarten. Multikulturelle Buntheit bietet sich dem Auge zwischen jungen Menschen und Familien, die diese größte innerstädtische Grünoase nutzen. Wie würde wohl die Hymne lauten, zu der er sich heute inspiriert fühlte?

With dour dignity Franz Stelzhamer (1802–1874), writer of the words to the Upper Austrian anthem, gazes into the Volksgarten. A multicoloured mix of cultures meets the eye as young people and families relax on this sprawling inner-city oasis of green. What would the anthem sound like if he were inspired to write it today?

PFLANZENFLÜSTERN

PLANT WHISPERS

Florale Ruhe hält über die ersten Herbsttage Einzug im Botanischen Garten. Im Orchideenhaus und in der Kakteensammlung sprießt und blüht es auf dem 4,2 Hektar großen Areal das ganze Jahr über.

In the first days of autumn floral calm descends on the Botanical Garden. But in the orchid house and the cactus collection, budding and blooming goes on all the year round on the 4.2-hectare grounds.

GEMEINSAM STARK – DIE TOP 4 IN LINZ!

STRENGTH IN NUMBERS – THE TOP 4 IN LINZ!

Grüne Mitte – BRW und Familie

Geballtes Know-how: BRW Baureform Wohnstätte, Familie, Lebensräume und VLW Vereinigte Linzer Wohnungsgenossenschaften – ein starker Verbund, der einerseits für innovativen Wohnbau mit Wohlfühlcharakter steht und andererseits sich dafür einsetzt, dass Wohnen leistbar bleibt.

Über Jahrzehnte hinweg in einem immerwährenden Lernprozess sind so die „Top 4 in Linz" entstanden.

- BRW Baureform Wohnstätte gegründet 1910
- Familie gegründet 1912
- Lebensräume gegründet 1909
- VLW Vereinigte Linzer Wohnungsgenossenschaften gegründet 1941

Combined expertise: BRW Baureform Wohnstätte, Familie, Lebensräume and VLW Vereinigte Linzer Wohnungsgenossenschaften form a potent alliance that stands for innovative housing and at the same time works to ensure that it remains affordable.

In this way the "top 4 in Linz" emerged from a constant learning process that has gone on for decades.

- *BRW Baureform Wohnstätte founded in 1910*
- *Familie founded in 1912*
- *Lebensräume founded in 1909*
- *VLW Vereinigte Linzer Wohnungsgenossenschaften founded in 1941*

Eisenhandstraße 22 – BRW

City Spot, Weingartshofstraße 23 – Lebensräume

Kleinmünchen, Sommerstraße 30 – VLW

AUENLAND

WATER MEADOWS

Naturnah lässt es sich im Europaschutzgebiet Traun-Donau-Auen wandern, dabei wilde Orchideen und seltene Krebsscheren erkunden. Die Weikerlseen fügen der Vielfalt des Linzer Stadtgebietes die wohl idyllischste Facette hinzu.

Hikes close to nature can be taken through the Traun-Danube water meadows, a European protection area, where wild orchids and rare water soldiers await discovery. The Weikerlseen give the city of Linz what is probably its most idyllic facet.

STADTSTRAND
CITY BEACH

Ferner, als sie ist, erscheint die Stadt am nachsommerlichen Pichlinger See. Die einstige Schottergrube hat sich zu einem ebenso beliebten wie belebten Badeparadies entwickelt, das an heißen Sommertagen Zehntausende Linzer an den Stadtrand lockt.

At the Pichlinger See in late summer the city seems further away than it really is. The former quarry has become a popular and bustling paradise for swimmers, attracting tens of thousands to the outskirts of Linz on hot summer days.

WOHNEN IST LEBEN

WHERE YOU LIVE IS HOW YOU LIVE

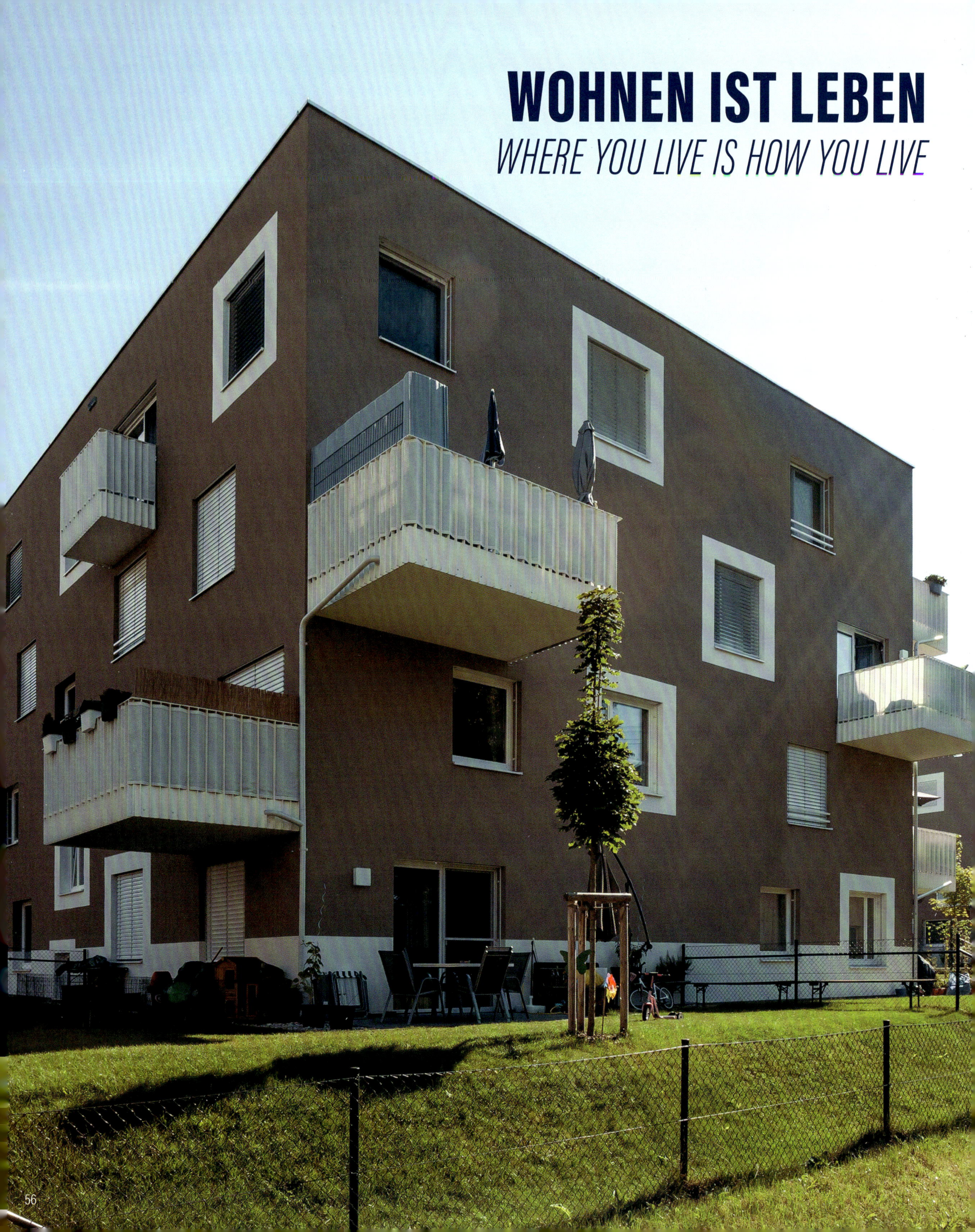

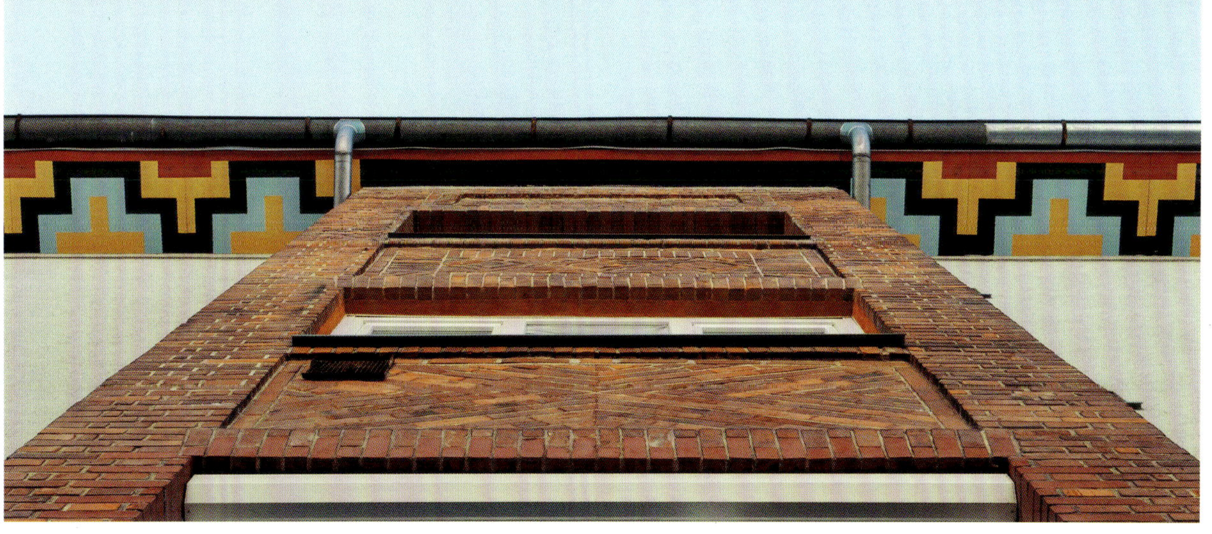

Mehr als die eigenen vier Wände, mehr als Zement und Ziegel sieht die GWG als gemeinnütziger Bauträger im Wohnen. Innovative Ideen schaffen neue Wohnwelten. Sie reichen von der Anpassung an eine veränderte Arbeitswelt bis zum digitalen Hausbesorger.

As a non-profit housebuilder, GWG sees more than a resident's "own four walls", more than bricks and mortar. Innovative ideas create new worlds of living. They range from adaptations to a changing working life to "digital concierges".

PANOPTIKUM

PANOPTICON

Der stille Bruder des Pöstlingbergs ist der Freinberg auf der gegenüberliegenden Seite der Donau. Schon in der Jungsteinzeit besiedelt, bildet er eine Keimzelle der Stadt. Von der Franz-Josefs-Warte schweift der Blick fast 100 Kilometer weit in die hochalpinen Regionen des Toten Gebirges.

Freinberg is the more peaceful brother of the Pöstlingberg on the opposite side of the Danube. Already a settlement in Neolithic times, it forms a nucleus of the city. The Franz-Josef tower offers views stretching almost 100 kilometres to the high alpine regions of the Totes Gebirge.

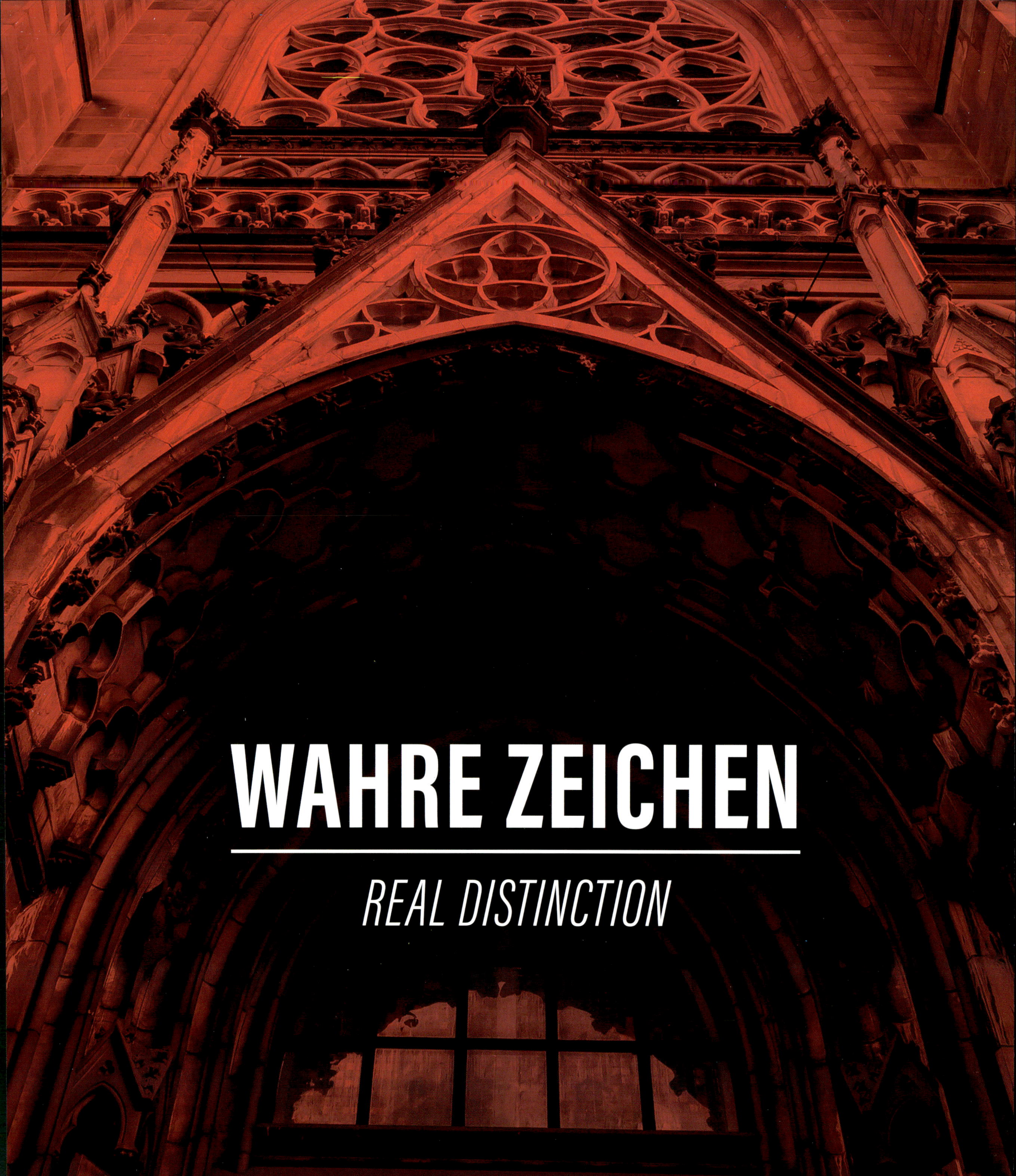

WAHRE ZEICHEN

REAL DISTINCTION

1.2

Wann hat man je in der Leere solche Fülle gesehen? Durch die 77 Glasfenster des Linzer Mariendoms flutet das Licht in königsblauen Streifen und kirschroten Zirkeln in den größten Kirchenraum Österreichs. Wären alle 20.000 da, die hier Platz finden: Niemand könnte sich dieser Art der Erleuchtung entziehen.

Has such profusion ever been seen in an empty space? Royal blue rays of light and cherry-red circles flood into Austria's largest church interior through the 77 glass windows of Linz's New Cathedral. Were all 20,000 people here that the cathedral can seat, none would be able to escape this brand of enlightenment.

Dabei ist der Mariendom geradezu ein „Neubau" unter den europäischen Kathedralen. Der Grundstein wurde erst 1862 gelegt und der Schlussstein 1934 gesetzt. Selbst spirituell sind die Linzer mit ihrem Dom ihrem Stil treu geblieben: Neugotisch aufstrebend, bleibt er dem Diesseits und der Gegenwart zugewandt. Die berühmten Glasfenster porträtieren zeitgenössische Würden-, Kron- und Entscheidungsträger in fotografischer Präzision und plastischen Szenen. Manche Besucher entdecken darauf einen Urgroßvater oder eine Urtante.

Von den Höhen des Doms fällt der Blick direkt ins touristische Schatzkästchen von Linz. Fast schon dörflich freundlich der Fassadenturm der Stadtpfarrkirche. Kaum zwanzig Jahre nach ihrer barocken Neuerrichtung haben seinerzeit die Jesuiten wenige Schritte entfernt den mächtigen Alten Dom ins Stadtbild gefügt – als „War Room" gegen den damals grassierenden Protestantismus. Gedämpft dringt das gelassene Getriebe des verkehrsberuhigten Stadtkerns herauf: vom mächtigen Geviert des barocken Hauptplatzes, einem der größten umbauten Plätze Europas. Aus dem Gassengewirr der Altstadt. Die Flanier- und Shopping-Meile der Landstraße zeichnet sich als feine Linie im Meer der Dächer ab.

Und weil diese Stadt stets zu Höherem berufen ist, hebt sich die Szenerie. Über das Linzer Schloss mit dem größten Universalmuseum Österreichs hinauf zu den granitenen Höhen der Wallfahrtskirche Pöstlingberg. Generationen von Firmlingen und Brautleuten haben an ihrem großen Tag den Blick auf Linz genossen. Von dort oben, wo der Neue Dom wie ein kühner Anker wirkt in einer Stadt, die stets der Zukunft entgegenfliegt.

Yet the Cathedral of the Immaculate Conception is a mere "youngster" among European cathedrals. The foundation stone was laid in 1862, the last one in 1934. With their cathedral the people of Linz have stayed true to their nature even in spiritual matters: rising up in the neo-Gothic style it remains focused on the here and now. The famous stained glass windows portray dignitaries, monarchs and decision-makers of the age with photographic precision and in vivid scenes. Some visitors even recognise a great-grandfather or ancestral aunt in them.

From the cathedral heights the eye falls directly on Linz's tourist treasure trove. The tower fronting the Stadtpfarrkirche has an almost rural charm. Barely twenty years after it was rebuilt in the Baroque style the Jesuits added the mighty Old Cathedral only a stone's throw away – as a bulwark against the Protestant religion that was rampant at the time. Up here, the hum of the traffic-calmed city centre is muffled: from the imposing rectangle of the Baroque main square, one of the largest enclosed squares in Europe. From the old town's labyrinthine lanes. Landstrasse, the promenade and shopping mile, is clearly visible as a clean line amid the sea of roofs.

And since this city is always destined to reach greater heights, the landscape rises too. Up past Linz Castle with Austria's largest universal museum to the granite heights of the pilgrimage church on the Pöstlingberg. Generations of candidates for confirmation and happy couples have enjoyed the view of Linz on their big day. From up there where the New Cathedral looks like a bold anchor in a city constantly flying towards the future.

Ein großes Herz beweist Linz mit seinem Hauptplatz. Im Zentrum des historischen Stadtkerns gelegen, gilt er als einer der größten umbauten Plätze Europas. „Gehen und gesehen werden" lautet die Devise, egal ob bei kulturellen Großveranstaltungen, beim Christkindlmarkt oder beim abendlichen Promenieren.

With its main square, Linz proves it has a big heart. Located right in the middle of the historic city centre it is one of Europe's largest enclosed squares. The motto here is "see and be seen", whether it is at major cultural events, at the Christmas market or on an evening stroll.

STADT DER BÜRGER

A CITY FOR ITS CITIZENS

Wahre Linzer begegnen auf dem Flanierkorso zwischen Dreifaltigkeitssäule und Neptunbrunnen am Hauptplatz nahen und entfernten Freunden. Manchmal auch dem Bürgermeister.

On the boulevard between the Holy Trinity column and the Neptune fountain on the main square, true citizens of Linz meet close friends and casual acquaintances. And occasionally the mayor.

MAGNÆ CŒLORUM DOMINÆ
INTEMERATÆ MATRI VIRGINI
MARIÆ
SINE LABE CONCEPTÆ
ORANTI MULTUM PRO POPULO
ET UNIVERSA CIVITATE
DIVIS HOSPITALIBUS
CAROLO

„DANKE" IN MARMOR

"THANK YOU" IN MARBLE

Weißer Salzburger Marmor, zwanzig Meter hoch: Wo vormals der Pranger stand, errichteten die Linzer 1716 auf dem Hauptplatz die opulent ausgeführte Dreifaltigkeitssäule. Dreifaltig waren mit der letzten Pestwelle, den Türken und dem Spanischen Erbfolgekrieg auch die Gefahren, anlässlich deren glimpflichen Ausgangs sie ein Zeichen des Dankes setzt.

White Salzburg marble, twenty metres high: Where once the pillory stood, the townsfolk of Linz placed the opulent Holy Trinity Column on the main square in 1716. Threefold were also the perils the city had faced: the last plague epidemic, the Turks and the War of the Spanish Succession. Since all were less deadly than feared, a sign of thanks was erected.

VOG

IM DIENSTE DES HANDELS

SERVING TRADE

Genuss verbindet. Mit Standorten in Europa wie in Asien ist die VOG Gruppe zu einer internationalen Drehscheibe im Lebensmittelgeschäft gewachsen. Und über Marken wie Lenz Moser Wein und Rapso – 100%ig reines Rapsöl – zu einem weltweiten Botschafter österreichischer Qualität. Gegründet 1916 im Gebäude Rathausgasse 1, hält das Unternehmen auch als internationaler Player dem Standort Linz seit mehr als einem Jahrhundert die Treue.

(A) good taste brings people together. With offices in Europe and Asia, the VOG Group has grown to become an international hub of the food industry. Brands such as Lenz Moser wine and Rapso – 100% pure rapeseed oil – have also made the holding a worldwide ambassador of Austrian quality. Founded in 1916 at Rathausgasse 1, the company has stayed loyal to Linz for over a century, even as an international player.

KOPFSACHE

HEADWAY

Die Brückenkopfgebäude zwischen Hauptplatz und Nibelungenbrücke spiegeln den modernen Weg der Stadt: von der neoklassizistischen Wucht der NS-Zeit zu einem offenen Haus samt Panoramalift und zum Quartier der Linzer Kunstuniversität.

The bridgehead buildings between the main square and the Nibelungenbrücke over the Danube reflect the city's modern orientation: from the neoclassical pomp of the Nazi era to a welcoming building with a panorama lift and the home of the University of Art and Design Linz.

RAT & TAT

WORDS AND DEEDS

Im Alten Rathaus geht es jünger zu, als es klingt: Die Linzer Stadtverwaltung gilt als eine der modernsten Österreichs. Und als eine der ältesten. Hinter der Renaissance-Fassade aus den Anfängen des 16. Jahrhunderts verbergen sich funktionelle Büros und Säle samt einem Pressezentrum auf dem neuesten technischen Stand.

At the Old Town Hall things are really not that old at all: the local government of Linz is considered one of the most modern in Austria. And one of the oldest. The Renaissance facade from the early days of the 16th century conceals functional offices and rooms as well as a press centre with state-of-the-art facilities.

GLOCKENSPIEL
RINGING TONES

Mozart, Haydn oder die Landeshymne begleitet zu festgesetzten Zeiten das Klappern von Gläsern und Tellern in den Schanigärten. Neben der prächtigen frühbarocken Fassade verdankt das Feichtinger-Haus – die vormalige Hofdruckerei und Verlagsanstalt Josef Feichtingers Erben – ihren Ruhm dem 1982 vom Kiwanis-Club gestifteten Glockenspiel.

The clatter of glasses and crockery in restaurant gardens is accompanied at fixed times by Mozart, Haydn or the Upper Austrian anthem. The fame of the Feichtinger House – once the home of the court printing press and the publishers Josef Feichtingers Erben – rests not only on its magnificent early Baroque facade but also on the carillon donated in 1982 by the Kiwanis Club.

FEINE TEXTUR

FINE FABRICS

Dekorativ gearbeitete Decken und mächtige Kastenfenster adeln das ehemalige Herrenhaus Löwenfeld & Hofmann zum baulichen Schmuckstück. Als Nachfolger der einstigen „Baumwollspinnerei" – sie hatte das Gebäude 1852 erworben – hat die Linz Textil Holding eine aufwendige Sanierung durchgeführt. Und präsentiert sich selbst in bester Form: Das Unternehmen ist Europas führender Hersteller von Garnen, Geweben und Frottierwaren.

Decorative ceilings and imposing box-type windows make the former Löwenfeld & Hofmann mansion an architectural gem. As successor to the former cotton mill that had bought the building in 1852, Linz Textil Holding carried out extensive refurbishment. And now presents itself from its best side: the company is Europe's leading manufacturer of yarns, fabrics and terry towelling.

LUXUS FÜR ALLE

LUXURY FOR ALL

Designhotels haben frische Akzente in das Linzer Beherbergungsangebot gebracht. Allen voran die „spinnerei", die lean luxury verspricht – und zu schlanken Preisen hält: mit junger, pfiffiger Architektur, die vom digitalen Self-Check-in bis zum superschnellen WiFi der „Generation 5G" ein Zuhause gibt.

Design hotels have brought fresh ideas to the range of hotel accommodation in Linz. In particular the "spinnerei" which promises lean luxury – with pared-down prices to match: youthful, eye-catching architecture, a digital self check-in and superfast Wi-Fi give the "5G generation" a place to feel at home.

GOTTESBURG

GOD'S STRONGHOLD

Streng erhebt sich der Alte Dom über das bunte Treiben der Linzer Innenstadt. Gegründet als barocke Landmark des hier einst mächtigen Jesuitenordens, diente er ab 1775 als Bischofskirche. Die mächtige Kanzel lässt den flammenden Charakter der hier gehaltenen Predigten noch erahnen.

The Old Cathedral towers austerely above the hustle and bustle of Linz city centre. Founded as the Baroque landmark of the Jesuit order, which once wielded great power here, it served as the episcopal church from 1775. The mighty pulpit still hints at the fiery nature of the sermons held on it.

Evangelische Pf

BEKENNTNIS ZUR VIELFALT

PROFESSING DIVERSITY

In allen Glauben vereint. Inmitten der allgegenwärtigen katholischen Tradition ragt nächst der Altstadt die Martin-Luther-Kirche auf, die mit einem direkt verlaufenden Straßenzug mit der Moschee der bosnischen Gemeinschaft verbunden ist. Wo es um Bekenntnisse geht, legt das moderne Linz ein Bekenntnis zur Vielfalt ab. Weil hier jeder Fortschritt damit beginnt, über die Unterschiede zum Gemeinsamen zu finden.

Meeting faith to faith. In the midst of the ubiquitous Catholic tradition, the Martin Luther Church towers beside the old town from which a street leads directly to the mosque of the Bosnian community. When it comes to faith, modern-day Linz professes diversity. Because here progress of every type begins by finding common ground through differences.

EIN LAND ALS HAUS

A LAND AS A HOUSE

Schattige Arkaden und heitere Renaissance machen das Landhaus zu einem Quell der Erquickung in der geschäftigen Innenstadt. Hier haben einst die oberennsischen Stände getagt, hier berät seit 1861 der Oberösterreichische Landtag. Der Arkadenhof mit dem „Planetenbrunnen" gilt als einer der schönsten Renaissance-Innenhöfe Österreichs.

Shady arcades and cheery Renaissance architecture make the Landhaus a source of uplift amid the bustle of the city centre. The estates from the region above the river Enns once held council here, and since 1861 it has been the seat of the Upper Austrian government. The arcade court with the "fountain of the planets" is regarded as one of Austria's finest Renaissance courtyards.

LÄSSIG BIS LUXURIÖS

FROM COSY TO CLASSY

Wohnungsvielfalt hat in Linz längst architektonische Einheitskost abgelöst. Bei Projektas als einem der präsentesten Immobilienvermarkter vor Ort hat Wohnen so viele Gesichter wie die Stadt selbst: das geförderte Eigenheim in der Vorstadt neben dem Familiendomizil am „Speckgürtel" und der Villa auf dem Freinberg. Oder der behagliche Altbau in Sichtweite eines jener smarten Hochhäuser, in denen es sich hoch über dem urbanen Treiben gleichsam schwerelos wohnen lässt ...

In Linz, faceless and indistinguishable architecture has long since given way to diversity in housing. At Projektas, one of the most prominent property marketers in Linz, housing has as many faces as the city itself: subsidised private housing in the suburbs, the family home in the commuter belt and the villa on Freinberg. Then there's the cosy old building within sight of one of the smart high-rises with homes far above the urban bustle where living seems weightless...

DICHTERFÜRST

PRINCE OF POETS

Ein Hauch Böhmerwald umweht das lebensgroße Denkmal von Adalbert Stifter (1805–1868). Der naturverbundene „Dichter der leisen Töne" hat als Landesschulinspektor in Linz residiert. Der Fels, der den Sockel des Denkmals bildet, wurde 1902 eigens aus dem Böhmerwald herangeschafft.

A hint of the Bohemian Forest surrounds the life-size statue of Adalbert Stifter (1805–1868). The nature-loving "poet of the gentle voice" lived in Linz as regional superintendent of schools. The rock upon which the statue rests was brought from the Bohemian Forest especially for the purpose in 1902.

ALTER SCHMUCK

OLD JEWEL

Als Rokoko-Juwel über die Grenzen des Landes hinaus gilt die Minoritenkirche. Sie war Teil des historischen Minoritenklosters: 1236 gegründet, repräsentierte es das erste und bedeutendste Kloster der Stadt, das weite Teile des heutigen Landhaus-Areals einnahm.

The Minoritenkirche is regarded in Upper Austria and beyond as a Rococo gem. The church was part of the historic monastery of the Friars Minor: founded in 1236, this was the city's first and most important monastery, covering much of the site now occupied by the Landhaus.

KAISERDOMIZIL

IMPERIAL RESIDENCE

Dramen haben sich im Kremsmünsterer Stiftshaus in der Altstadt abgespielt. Habsburger-Kaiser Friedrich III. entschied hier über Wohl und Wehe des deutsch-römischen Reiches. Und starb 1493 hinter diesen Mauern – angeblich nach dem „übermäßigen Verzehr von Melonen". Wenige Jahre später wurde der mächtige Renaissance-Bau vom Stift Kremsmünster erworben.

Dramas have been played out in the Kremsmünster Abbey's former townhouse. It was here that Habsburg emperor Frederick III presided over the weal and woe of the Holy Roman Empire. And it was behind these walls that he died in 1493 – allegedly of "a surfeit of melons". A few years later the imposing Renaissance building was purchased by Kremsmünster Abbey.

linz
KREMSMÜNSTERERHAUS
Seit 1507 Stiftshaus
Neubau 1579/80, Umbau 1585/86
Erhöhung und Rund-Erkern
1616

AM PFARRPLATZ

ON PFARRPLATZ

Dörflicher Charme ist es geradezu, den die Linzer Stadtpfarrkirche ausstrahlt. Nur wenige Schritte östlich des belebten Hauptplatzes prägen hier Ruhe und Beschaulichkeit den Pfarrplatz. Dabei gehört der 84 Meter hohe Glockenturm zu den charakteristischen Akzenten in der Silhouette der Stadt.

Linz Stadtpfarrkirche exudes the sort of charm more often found in villages. Just a stone's throw to the east of the busy main square, Pfarrplatz is a place where peace and tranquillity prevail. The 84-metre-high bell tower is one of the distinctive features of the city's skyline.

SCHLOSSBERG

SCHLOSSBERG

Urbanität und Idylle gehen auf dem Linzer Schlossberg Hand in Hand. In nächster Nähe zum Stadtzentrum werden hier die Geräusche leiser, die Gärten größer und wird die Szenerie weiter. Beseelt von der gleichmäßigen Ruhe des Donaustroms, der sich von hier oben dem Blick darbietet.

On the Schlossberg in Linz, urbanity and idyllic scenery go hand in hand. Here, a stone's throw from the city centre, sounds are quieter, gardens bigger and the views longer. Infused with the calm of the smooth-flowing Danube upon which the eye rests from up here.

FLUCHTBURG

REFUGE

Drei Habsburger haben hier Zuflucht gefunden: Friedrich III. vor dem Ungarnkönig Matthias Corvinus, Ferdinand III. vor der Pest und Leopold I. vor den Türken. Heute beherbergt das Linzer Schloss das größte Universalmuseum Österreichs. Die Terrasse des stilvollen Schlosscafés präsentiert Linz doppelt übersichtlich: „live" als Panorama-Ausblick und historisch als Stadtmodell.

Three Habsburgs found refuge here: Frederick III from the Hungarian king Matthias Corvinus, Ferdinand III from the plague and Leopold I from the Turks. Today, Linz Castle houses Austria's largest universal museum. The terrace of the elegant castle café offers an overview of Linz twice over: as a real-life panorama and as a model of the historical city.

1.000 JAHRE UND MEHR

1,000 YEARS AND COUNTING

Als älteste Kirche Österreichs galt die Martinskirche lange Zeit. Urkundlich belegt ist sie bereits seit dem Jahr 799. Vermutlich stand sie in direkter Verbindung zu den benachbarten Befestigungen des Schlosses. Im Inneren prägen der gotische Chor und einst farbenprächtige Fresken das Bild.

St. Martin's was long thought to be the oldest church in Austria. It is first documented as early as 799 and was probably linked to the fortifications adjacent to the castle. The interior is dominated by the Gothic choir and the once-colourful frescoes.

HIGH-LIGHTS

HIGH LIGHTS

Das Raumwunder des Mariendoms entfaltet mehr Kubatur als jenes des Wiener Stephansdoms, der Turm ist gerade zwei Meter niedriger. High-Lights im wörtlichen Sinne sind die berühmten Gemäldefenster. Sie erzählen Geschichten und bilden Menschen und Szenerien des historischen Linz in geradezu fotografischer Qualität ab.

The amazing space inside the Mariendom covers more cubic metres than St. Stephen's in Vienna, while its spire is only two metres lower. The famous stained glass windows are literally "high lights". They tell stories and show people and scenes from Linz's past in a quality bordering on the photographic.

HAUS AM DOM

HOTEL BY THE CATHEDRAL

Gastlich gleich vis-à-vis von Österreichs größtem Dom präsentiert sich das Hotel am Domplatz. Persönlich geführt und top ausgestattet bietet das erste Erwachsenenhotel der Region eine Oase der Ruhe unmittelbar in der Linzer Innenstadt. Mit im Wohlfühlpaket ist die Benutzung des kleinen, aber feinen Spa-Bereiches im Haus.

Hospitality right opposite Austria's biggest cathedral is offered by the Hotel am Domplatz. Personal service and first-class facilities are standard at the region's first adults-only hotel: an oasis of peace in the heart of Linz. The feel-good package includes use of the hotel's small but supremely relaxing spa area.

KREATIVBEZIRK

CREATIVE QUARTER

Regional bis experimentell sind die Events und Ausstellungen, die im OÖ Kulturquartier mit dem Landeskulturzentrum Ursulinenhof über die Bühne gehen. Hier findet die oberösterreichische Kulturszene ihren Dreh- und Angelpunkt. Zur touristischen Top-Marke hat es der „Höhenrausch" gebracht: Holztreppen und -brücken führen hoch über die Linzer Innenstadt und zu spannenden Kunstinstallationen.

The events and exhibitions staged in the Upper Austrian Kulturquartier in association with the Landeskulturzentrum Ursulinenhof range from the locally flavoured to the experimental. It is here that the Upper Austrian cultural scene finds its epicentre. "Höhenrausch" has become a top brand for tourists: wooden steps and bridges lead high up over Linz city centre to fascinating artistic installations.

KLOSTER-OPENING

A CONVENT OPENS UP

Standfest im Mahlstrom der Geschichte behauptet sich das vormalige Ursulinenkloster als architektonisches Kraftzentrum entlang der Landstraße. Erst 1968 wurde der Orden der Ursulinen hier aufgelassen. Das Land hat die Baulichkeiten erworben und als Kulturzentrum den Linzern geöffnet.

Impervious to the vagaries of history, the former convent of the Ursuline Sisters stands firm as an architectural powerhouse on Landstrasse. The Order of Saint Ursula lived and worked here until 1968. The Upper Austrian government then bought the complex and opened it to the people of Linz as a cultural centre.

Der LANGSCHLÄFER
ZWERGENKÖNIG

GROTTENGUT

ALL THE FUN OF THE FAIRY TALE

„Küssen verboten!" hat bis vor wenigen Jahrzehnten noch ein Schild in der Grottenbahn auf dem Pöstlingberg verordnet. Märchenhaft wirken Stimmung und Motive heute wie damals, zauberhaft wie aus einem Raimund-Stück die Atmosphäre in den historischen Überresten eines maximilianischen Wehrturms. Für Generationen von Oberösterreichern bildet die Drachen-, Hexen- und Zwergenwelt auf dem Pöstlingberg einen fixen Bestandteil ihrer kollektiven Erinnerung aus Kindheits- oder Jugendtagen.

"No kissing!" said a sign at the Grottenbahn on the Pöstlingberg until only a few decades ago. The fairy-tale atmosphere and figures weave the same magic today as the Dragon Express trundles through a fantastic world conjured up in the historic remains of a fortified tower from the days of Emperor Maximilian. For generations of Upper Austrians, the world of dragons, witches and dwarves on the Pöstlingberg is an integral part of their collective childhood memory.

TRINK, BRÜDERLEIN!

CHEERS!

Versteckt und Eingeweihten seit Jahrhunderten bekannt ist das „Heilige Bründl" am Fußweg zum Pöstlingberg. Die Naturgrotte, in der eine Quelle sprudelt, diente bereits in vorchristlicher Zeit als Kultstätte. Manche vermuten gar, dass der Wallfahrtsstatus des Pöstlingbergs auf sie zurückgeht.

Hidden away but known to insiders for centuries is the "Heiliges Bründl" on the path to the Pöstlingberg. This natural grotto with its spring was a place of worship as far back as pre-Christian times. There are even some who suspect that it is the origin of the hill as a place of pilgrimage.

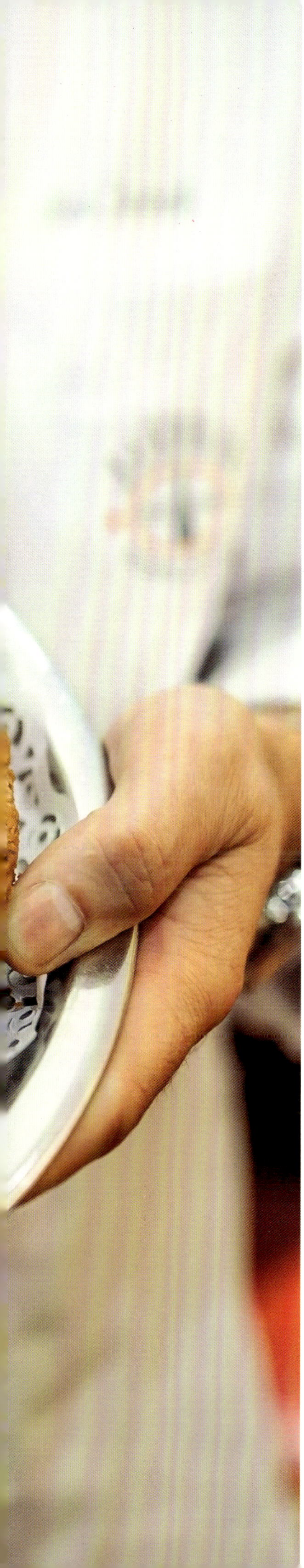

WELTÄLTESTE TORTE

WORLD'S OLDEST CAKE

Als süßeste Ikone der Stadt gilt die Linzer Torte. Fast schon ebenso bekannt wie die geschichtsträchtige Mehlspeise – die bereits 1653 in einem Kochbuch zu finden war – ist die Traditionskonditorei Jindrak. Neben dem Stammhaus der „Original Linzer Torte" in der Herrenstraße finden sich weitere Standorte in ganz Linz, unter anderem in bester Aussichtslage auf dem Pöstlingberg. Sie alle eint der unverwechselbare Duft von Mandeln, Haselnüssen, Butter, Ribiseln und Gewürzen.

The city's sweetest icon: that's Linzer torte. Almost as famous as the cake with its rich history – it was included in a cookbook way back in 1653 – is Jindrak, the traditional pastry makers. Besides the main café on Herrenstrasse where the "Original Linzer Torte" was born, the patisserie has branches all over Linz, like the one on the Pöstlingberg with its fantastic views. They all share the unmistakable aroma of almonds, hazelnuts, butter, redcurrants and spices.

WAHRES STREBEN

REAL EFFORTS

1.3

An den Uferpromenaden verweben sich bunte Radtrikots, lachende Stimmen und Grillduft von irgendwoher zum feinen Gespinst eines Sommernachmittags. Begleitet vom stoischen Strom der Donau, der dieser Stadt immer unbeirrbar Zug und Richtung gegeben hat.

On the riverside promenades, colourful cycling jerseys, the sound of laughter and the aroma of a barbecue somewhere or other mingle to weave the fine fabric of a summer's afternoon. Accompanied by the stoic flow of the Danube that has always unerringly taken the city forward and guided it.

Längst verbindet der Fluss, was er einst getrennt hat. Vom „armen Vetter" und der Heimstatt von Fischern und Schiffsleuten hat sich Urfahr am linken Donauufer zur Beletage von Linz gemausert. Mit den begehrtesten Immobilien der Stadt, mit zwei Universitäten als intellektuellem Zentrum über die Region hinaus. Zusammenhalt in der Vielfalt, Wohlstand und Lebensqualität, geistiger Aufbruch: Entlang der Nibelungenbrücke spannen Lentos und Ars Electronica Center die dominante kulturelle Achse der Stadt. Hier wird sichtbar und spürbar, was sich die Linzer in Generationen gemeinsam erarbeitet haben.

Lange zurück liegen die legendären Worte des damaligen Bürgermeisters Ernst Koref, mit denen er den Zustand der Stadt nach dem Zweiten Weltkrieg beschrieben hat: „Von der Barockstadt sind wir zur Barackenstadt geworden." Linz war großflächig zerstört und überlaufen von Flüchtenden und Entwurzelten.

Die Menschen in Linz haben die Herausforderung auf ihre Art angenommen: mit aufgekrempelten Ärmeln. Mit jenem unverbrüchlichen Glauben an die Zukunft, der sie stets eine neue Zukunft schaffen lässt: indem sie ihr industrielles Erbe aus einer unseligen Zeit neu angepackt und neu gestaltet haben. Indem sie mit beherztem Wohnbau den Linzerinnen und Linzern Raum gegeben haben. Später, in den 1990ern, mit einer konsequenten Verbesserung der Luftgüte auch der Freude an ihrer Stadt. Eine Freude, die zur kulturellen Öffnung und Reife der „Kulturhauptstadt Europas" des Jahres 2009 aufblühte. Und die heute im Selbstbild der „Future City of Respect" gipfelt. Es ist diese Freude am Leben und Machen, die sich in den Gesichtern der Jogger am Donauufer widerspiegelt.

What the river once kept apart it has long since connected. Urfahr, on the left bank of the Danube and in olden times the "country cousin" and home of fishermen and sailors, has blossomed into Linz's "piano nobile". With the city's most sought-after properties and two universities as an intellectual hub reaching beyond the region's borders. Togetherness amid diversity, prosperity and quality of life, pioneering intellectual work: along the Nibelungenbrücke, the Lentos Museum and Ars Electronica Center form the city's foremost cultural axis. Here, what the people of Linz have achieved together over the generations becomes visible and audible.

Many years have now passed since the former mayor, Ernst Koref, described the city's situation after World War II with the legendary words, "From a Baroque city we have become a barrack city." Large parts of Linz had been destroyed or were overrun by refugees and people who had lost their homes.

The people of Linz faced the challenge in their own particular way: by rolling up their sleeves. With that unshakeable faith in the future that repeatedly enables them to create a new one: they went to work on the industry they had inherited from a period of horror and remodelled it. They provided the citizens of Linz with living space by indefatigably building new homes. Later, in the 1990s, firm measures to improve the air quality also increased the inhabitants' pride in their city. Pride that blossomed into a cultural opening and maturity as "European Capital of Culture" in 2009. And which today culminates in Linz's image of itself as a "Future City of Respect". It is this enjoyment of life and achievement that is reflected in the faces of the joggers on the banks of the Danube.

RUNDUM VERSORGT

WELL PROVIDED FOR

Ob Strom, Gas und Wärme, Wasserversorgung, Abfall- und Abwasserentsorgung, ob Bäder, Friedhöfe oder der Hafen: Die LINZ AG kümmert sich um die hohe Lebens- und Businessqualität der Stadt. Damit selbstverständlich auch um den taktgenauen Verkehr der Öffis, mit denen ebenso das Kundenzentrum in der Wiener Straße und das LINIEN-Infocenter auf dem Hauptplatz erreichbar sind.

Electricity, gas and heating, water, waste and sewage disposal, plus swimming pools, cemeteries and the airport: LINZ AG makes sure the high quality of life and business in the city is maintained. It goes without saying that this also includes ensuring the punctuality of public transport, which also serves the customer centre on Wiener Strasse and the LINIEN information centre on the main square.

DIESE/S
AUF//ES
HUETZE
ROHLIC
ST/AUF

KRAFTWERK

POWER STATION

Voestalpine und LINZ AG bilden als die beiden führenden Investorinnen im Stadtgebiet gemeinsam das wirtschaftliche „Kraftwerk" in Linz. Beide haben sie eine Stadt maßgeblich mitgeformt, in der es sich heute ebenso lohnend arbeiten wie angenehm leben lässt.

Voestalpine and LINZ AG, the two leading investors in the city, form the economic "power station" in Linz. They have been instrumental in shaping a city which today is as much a pleasant place to work as it is to live.

WÄRMSTENS EMPFOHLEN

WARMLY RECOMMENDED

Wärme macht Meter: Rund drei von vier Haushalten in Linz vertrauen bei ihrem Wohnkomfort auf das städtische Fernwärmenetz. Das ist österreichweit ein Spitzenwert und zudem versorgungssicher und umweltfreundlich. Erzeugt wird die Wärme über die Dampfturbinen eigener Kraftwerke, bevorzugt mit nicht fossilen Brennstoffen wie Biomasse/Holz und Reststoffen.

Warmth covers ground: approximately three quarters of households in Linz trust the municipal district heating grid to provide their home comforts. This is among the highest percentages in Austria. What is more, this system is reliable and environmentally friendly. The heat is generated using steam turbines in dedicated power stations, wherever possible with non-fossil fuels such as biomass/wood and waste.

AM WASSER GEBAUT

BUILT ON WATER

Quellfrisch und dazu noch kostengünstig wie selten sonst wo in Europa ist das Trinkwasser der Linzer. Aus Brüssel gab es dafür Bestätigung und Auszeichnung. In der Parklandschaft der „Wasserwelt Scharlinz" werden 127 Jahre städtischer Wasserversorgung in einer multimedialen Ausstellung erlebbar. Das historische Wasserwerk vor Ort sorgt für einen Rahmen, wie er passender nicht sein könnte.

Drinking water in Linz comes fresh from the spring and costs less than in most of the rest of Europe into the bargain. Brussels has confirmed this, and presented an award for it. In the parkland containing "Wasserwelt Scharlinz" visitors can explore 127 years of municipal water supply in a multimedia exhibition. The historical waterworks there provides a location that could not be more appropriate.

UNTER WASSER

UNDER WATER

Unter dem Flussgrund führt der „Donaudüker" über 375 Meter von einem Ufer der Donau zum anderen. Er verbindet das Linzer Stadtgebiet mit der Nachbargemeinde Steyregg. Neben Frischwasser, Abwasser und Strom führt der 1974 in Betrieb genommene Düker auch Fußgänger: Die Führungen gelten als Geheimtipp unter Erkundungsfreudigen!

The "Donaudüker" is a "culvert" under the riverbed, 375 metres long and linking one bank of the Danube to the other. It links the city of Linz with the neighbouring town of Steyregg. The tunnel, opened in 1974, carries not only fresh water, sewage and electricity, but pedestrians as well. Guided tours of it are an insiders' tip for novelty-seekers.

Donner
Oktober

KIND SEIN MIT ALLEN SINNEN

CHILDHOOD FOR ALL THE SENSES

Ob Krabbelstube, Tagesmutter oder Omadienst, Kindergarten oder Hort: Linz hat das Angebot an Kinderbetreuung ausgebaut wie wenige Städte sonst. Die Förderung der Kinder in allen Bereichen ihrer Entwicklung ist die Leitidee, an denen sich Pläne, Gebäude und pädagogische Konzepte orientieren. Zum Wohl der Kinder und ihrer Eltern, zum Nutzen des Lebens- und Wirtschaftsstandortes.

Crèche, child minder or granny, kindergarten or after-school care: few other towns have expanded their childcare facilities as much as Linz. The guiding principle behind the schemes, buildings and educational concepts is the promotion of every aspect of children's development. So that children and their parents benefit and the city as a place to live and work profits too.

BÄRENSTARK

BEAR ESSENTIALS

In der Spezies „ursidae" zählen sie neben Schwarzbär und Pandabär schon seit 1922 weltweit zu den wichtigsten Vertretern: die Goldbären von Haribo. Von ihrem Kern-Habitat in Linz aus besiedeln sie den ost- und südeuropäischen Raum. Seit 1989 wird im Linzer Werk täglich eine Vielzahl von Varianten des Kult-Fruchtgummis produziert.

Since 1922 they have been among the world's most prominent members of the Ursidae family alongside the black bear and the giant panda: the Haribo Goldbears. They spread out from their core habitat in Linz to occupy territories in eastern and southern Europe. Since 1989 the Linz factory has been turning out a wide variety of fruit gums on a daily basis.

FLUSSAUFWÄRTS

UPSTREAM

Die Seele weit ausbreiten. Die Nähe der Stadt atmen, das Grün der Wiesen aufsaugen, die Kraft des Flusses spüren. Dazu bevölkern die Linzer an sonnigen Tagen gerne die Uferpromenaden rechts und links der Donau. Walkend, joggend oder radelnd. Allein oder mit Kind und Kegel. Im Liegestuhl, im Gastgarten oder auf der Picknickdecke.

Giving the soul room. Breathing in the nearby city, soaking up the green of the meadows, feeling the power of the river. This is what prompts the people of Linz to flock to the promenades on both sides of the river on sunny days. Walking, jogging or cycling. Alone or with the whole family. In a deckchair, in a beer garden or on a picnic blanket.

WOHNWERTE
LIVING VALUES

Die Kunst des Wohnens hat die Neue Heimat OÖ nicht zuletzt an zahlreichen Bauten in Linz über 80 Jahre zur Reife geführt. Der Mensch mit seiner Umwelt und Zukunft steht im Zentrum der Vision. So hat das gemeinnützige Unternehmen unter anderem den Energy Globe OÖ für seine Bemühungen um Effizienz und Nachhaltigkeit im Wohn- und Kommunalbau verliehen bekommen.

Neue Heimat Upper Austria has perfected the art of living over a period of 80 years, not least in countless residential buildings in Linz. At the heart of its vision are the environment and the future. This has won the non-profit company accolades such as the Upper Austrian Energy Globe for its efforts to achieve efficiency and sustainability in residential and municipal building construction.

1 - 7

AUF DER GUGL

AT THE GUGL

Schwarz und Weiß sind die Vereinsfarben des LASK. Zwischen Abstiegskampf und Champions-League-Play-off verläuft seine stolze Geschichte. 1965 setzte er sich als erster Nicht-Wiener Klub durch und holte den Meisterteller nach Hause auf die Linzer „Gugl". Der Anpfiff zum Umbau dieser traditionsreichen Linzer Sportstätte zu einem länderspieltauglichen Stadion nach modernsten Standards ist bereits erfolgt. Auch der Lokalrivale Blau-Weiß Linz, zuletzt 1974 österreichischer Fußballmeister, erhält im Donaupark eine moderne Heimstätte.

Black and white are the club colours of LASK. Both relegation battles and Champions League play-offs are part of its proud history. In 1965, LASK was the first club outside Vienna to win the league and the champions' trophy was brought home to their ground in Linz, the "Gugl". The refurbishment of this stadium steeped in tradition as a venue suitable for international matches that meets the very latest standards has already kicked off. A state-of-the-art ground is also being built in the Donaupark for their local rivals Blau-Weiss Linz, who last won the Austrian championship in 1974.

EISARENA

ICE RINK

Hitzig auf gefrorenem Boden geht es bisweilen in der LINZ AG Eisarena zu. „Volles Haus" ist angesagt, wenn die „Black Wings" zu einem Schlüsselspiel auslaufen: Die Linzer Spitzenmannschaft spielt in der multinationalen ICE Hockey League mit, hat zweimal den österreichischen Meistertitel geholt – und wurde 2009 als erste österreichische Mannschaft zu einem Turnier nach Nordamerika eingeladen.

Heated battles are played out on the frozen ice of the LINZ AG Eisarena. When the "Black Wings" run out onto the ice for a crunch game the place is packed to the rafters: The top Linz team plays in the multinational ICE Hockey League, has twice been crowned Austrian champions – and in 2009 became the first Austrian team to be invited to take part in a tournament in North America.

REAL 360
Steinbach
LINZ AG
bet-a
greiner

LINZ AG

STADTPRÄGEND

SHAPING THE CITY

Die Wohnstadt Linz hat gerade im sozialen Wohnbau international Akzente gesetzt. Die solide Wohnqualität und das Lebensgefühl etwa in Stadtteilen wie Bindermichl oder Spallerhof hat die WAG Wohnungsanlagen GmbH mitgeprägt. Und tut das heute weit über Linz hinaus, so wie mit diesem 80-jährigen Gebäude: Mit einer vorgesetzten Wandscheibe bietet es erweiterten Freiraum für die Bewohner. Als „Qualitätsanbieter in jedem Preissegment" besitzt die WAG rund 23.000 Wohnungen und verwaltet doppelt so viele in insgesamt fünf Bundesländern.

As a residential city, Linz has had an international impact with its public housing schemes. The firm of WAG Wohnungsanlagen GmbH has helped create the quality housing and pleasant ambience found in districts such as Bindermichl and Spallerhof. And does so today far beyond the borders of Linz, for instance with this 80-year-old building: an additional shear wall gives the residents more room to move. As a "provider of quality housing in every price category" WAG owns around 23,000 properties and manages twice as many in five provinces.

DRI

DIE ZUKUNFT LIEGT IN DER UNGEDULD.

THE FUTURE RELIES ON IMPATIENCE.

DAS SCHWERE UND DAS SCHNELLE

THE HEAVY AND THE FAST

2.1

Irreal mutet die vormittägliche Ruhe auf der Aussichtsplattform der Stahlwelt voestalpine an. Gelassen zeichnet „Hochofen A" zackige Konturen in den Himmel. Die schmale Dampfwolke kommt vom Chemiepark nebenan. Nichts lässt das produktive Inferno im Inneren dieses Industriemolochs erahnen, wo bei weit über 2.000° Celsius Stahl gekocht wird.

The mid-morning calm on the observation platform of the voestalpine Stahlwelt has something unreal about it. "Blast furnace A" serenely traces a jagged outline against the sky. The thin plume of steam comes from the adjacent Chemiepark. Nothing hints at the productive inferno in the bowels of this industrial colossus where steel is boiled at temperatures well over 2,000 °C.

Trügerisch war die Ruhe nahe der Mündung des Traunflusses in die Donau immer schon. Noch in den 1930er-Jahren herrschte hier die dörfliche Idylle von St. Peter-Zizlau. Bis die NS-Machthaber ab 1938 im Eilverfahren Bauernhäuser mit ihren Gärten, die Kirche samt Schule und die beliebten Gastwirtschaften in Spazierweite der Linzer schliffen, das Gelände aufschütteten und hier einen Stahl- und Chemiekomplex von europäischem Rang hochzogen.

Die Linzer haben nach dem Zweiten Weltkrieg daraus das Rückgrat der österreichischen Industrie geformt und zur Zeit des Wiederaufbaus die Hochburg der „Verstaatlichten". Beliefert von dampfenden Zügen voll mit Rohstoffen vom steirischen Erzberg. Beflügelt von Innovationen wie dem LD-Verfahren, das die Stahlproduktion weltweit revolutioniert hat. Angespornt vom rasanten Aufstieg der Stadt zum stärksten Industriestandort Österreichs.

Eine Rolle, die Linz heute unangefochten behauptet. Die voestalpine AG hat sich zu einem weltweit erfolgreichen Hersteller von Stahlspezialitäten transformiert. Weitere Leitbetriebe aus der Bau-, der Energie- und der IT-Branche prägen das industrielle wie das internationale Profil der Stadt. Sie haben den Nährboden geschaffen für schnelle, innovative Klein- und Mittelbetriebe des Typs „Industrie 4.0". Dazu verleihen dem Linz von heute boomende Dienstleistungen und mittlerweile ein Platz unter den Top 3 der Kongressstädte in Österreich jenen Glamour, der der Industriestadt von gestern fernlag.

The peace near where the river Traun meets the Danube has always been deceptive. Until the 1930s the area was a rural idyll around the village of St. Peter-Zizlau. But in 1938 the Nazi rulers began summarily tearing down the farmhouses with their gardens, the church and school, and the much-loved inns within walking distance of the city of Linz. The site was filled in and a steelmaking and chemical complex of European standing constructed.

After the end of World War II the people of Linz turned it into the backbone of Austrian industry and, during the period of reconstruction, a stronghold for nationalised industry. It was supplied by steaming trains laden with ore from the Erzberg mountain in Styria. Bolstered by innovations like the LD process that revolutionised steelmaking worldwide. Spurred on by the city's meteoric rise to become Austria's foremost industrial location.

A position that remains undisputed to this day. voestalpine AG has transformed itself into a globally successful producer of specialist steels. Other leading companies in the construction, energy and IT branches give the city its industrial and international identity. They have created the breeding ground for fast, innovative small and medium-sized Industry 4.0 enterprises. A booming service sector and the city's rise into the top three congress cities in Austria lend today's Linz the glamour that the industrial town of yesteryear never had.

STAHLWELT

WORLD OF STEEL

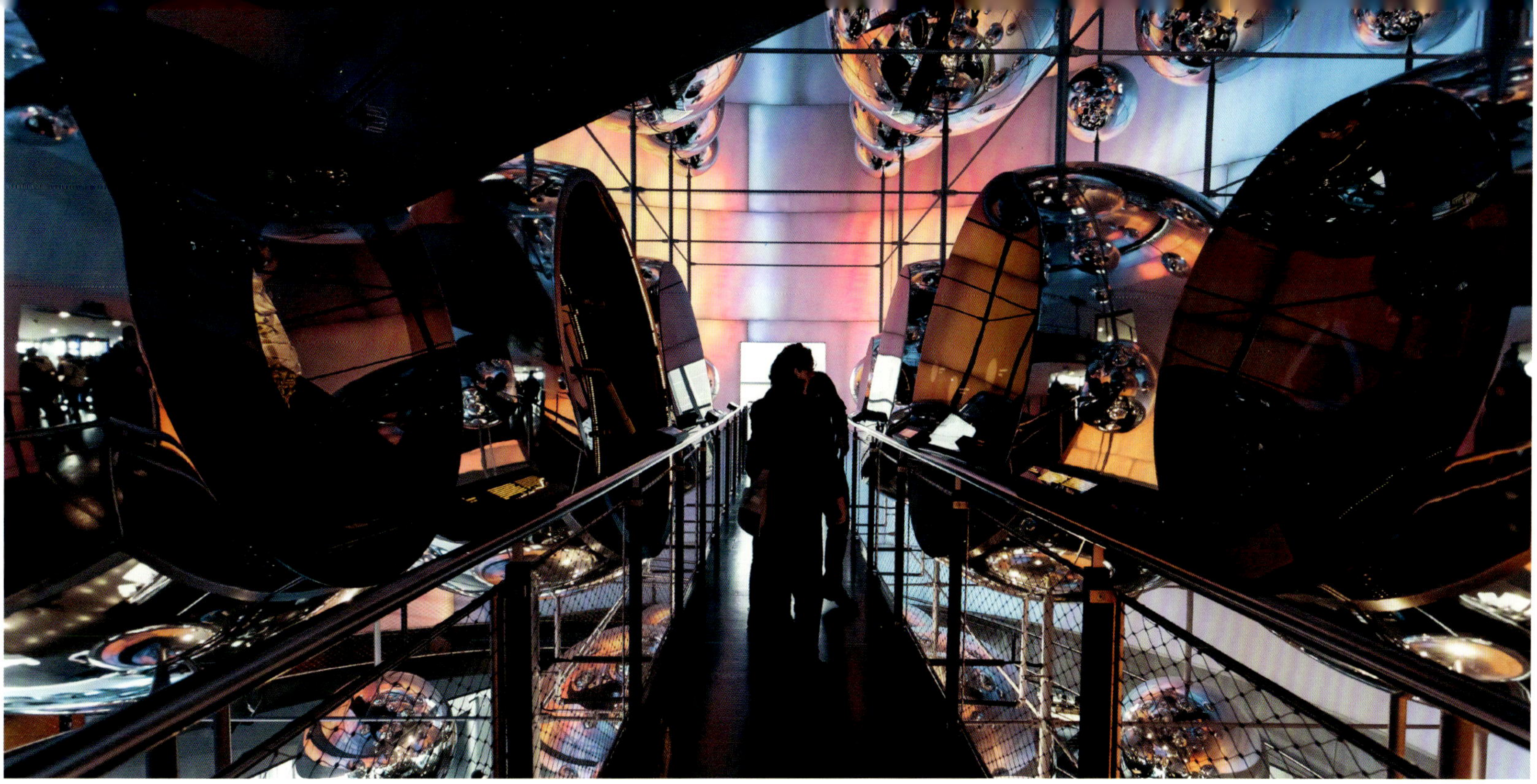

Interaktiv lässt sich die Welt des Stahls in der voestalpine Stahlwelt erleben. Zwischen 80 mächtigen Stahlrotunden entfaltet sich auf mehreren Ebenen das Panorama von Österreichs führendem Industriekonzern, der fast 50.000 Menschen in mehr als 50 Ländern der Erde beschäftigt. Den eindrucksvollen Abschluss bildet der Blick von der Panorama-Terrasse auf Hochöfen, Gasometer und das futuristische Verwaltungsgebäude.

The voestalpine Stahlwelt offers an interactive way to discover the world of steel. Between 80 huge steel rotundas an all-round view of Austria's leading industrial concern – which today employs nearly 50,000 people in over 50 countries – unfolds on several levels. A view of the blast furnaces, the gasometer and the futuristic office complex provides an impressive finale.

VIVATIS
www.vivatis.at

MARKENKRAFT
STRONG BRANDS

Made in A, managed in Linz: Hochwertige Rohstoffe aus Österreich bilden die Grundlage für die VIVATIS HOLDING AG als eines der größten heimischen Unternehmen der Nahrungs- und Genussmittelbranche. Im Portfolio finden sich Markenklassiker, die Generationen verbinden, aber auch den Geist der Zeit spiegeln: etwa über eine moderne Produktion, die Ressourcen sparsam einsetzt und Strom ausschließlich aus nachhaltigen Quellen bezieht.

Made in A, managed in Linz: high-quality raw materials from Austria form the basis of the VIVATIS HOLDING AG as one of Austria's biggest players in the food and beverage industry. The portfolio includes classic brands that are loved by generations but also reflect the spirit of the times, for example by using modern production techniques that save resources and by only using power from sustainable sources.

POWERED BY SIEMENS ENERGY

POWERED BY SIEMENS ENERGY

Transformatoren für die Welt fertigt Siemens Energy am Standort Linz-Kraußstraße. Mit cloudbasiertem Monitoring und alternativen Isolierstoffen bietet das Linzer Werk zukunftssichere Lösungen. Das Bürogebäude wirkt heute unscheinbar und ist doch historisch markant: 1953 errichtet, gilt es als das erste Hochhaus der Stadt.

Siemens Energy on Kraussstrasse in Linz manufactures transformers for the world. With cloud-based monitoring and alternative insulating materials the Linz plant provides future-safe solutions. Today the office building appears to be nothing special, and yet it has historical significance: when it was built in 1953 it was the first high-rise building in the city.

Fluke 175 Nr.9
Nr.10
SUMMATION
62204762
VNB

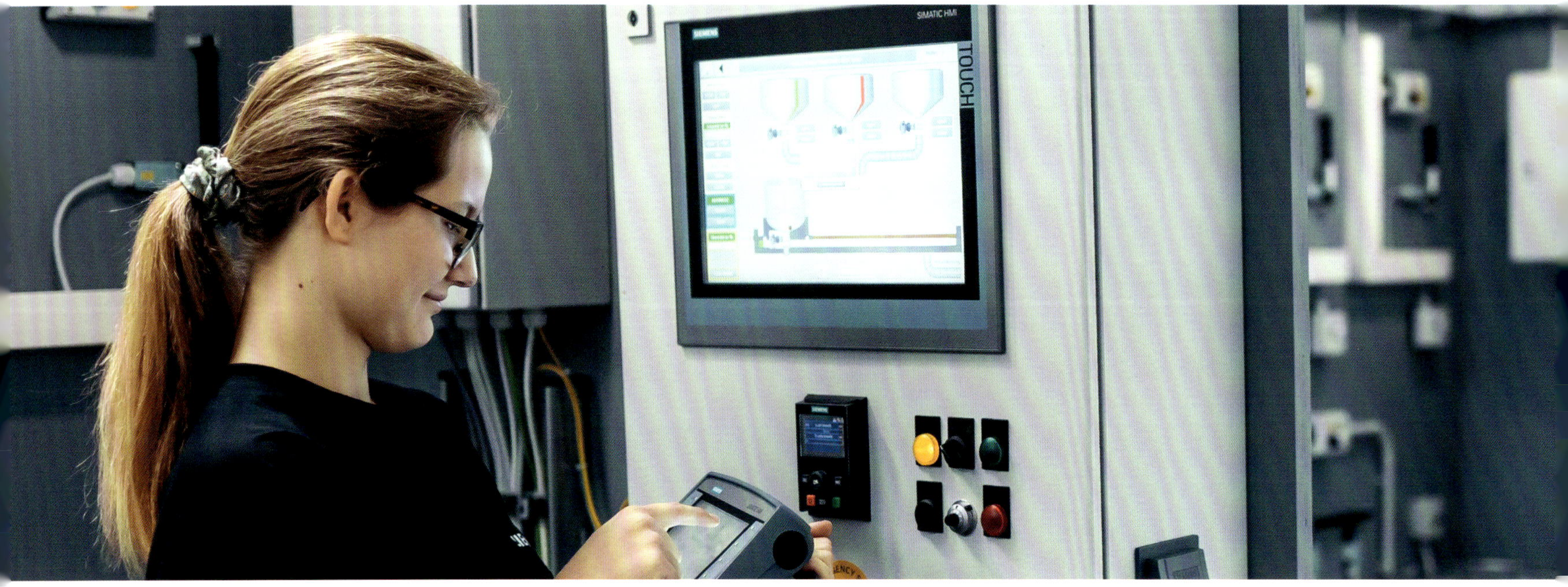
SIMATIC HMI
TOUCH

POWERED BY SIEMENS

POWERED BY SIEMENS

Siemens Linz verkörpert geradezu die frühzeitige Vision auf dem Weg zur Industrie 4.0. Hier wird Zukunft gestaltet: im weltweiten Siemens-Headquarter zur Entwicklung hochkomplexer Automatisierung für die Auto- und Luftfahrtindustrie. Dabei lässt sich durchaus von „gewachsenen Qualitäten" sprechen: Das erste technische Büro hat Siemens schon 1902 in Linz eröffnet. Heute setzt Siemens Oberösterreich darüber hinaus Akzente in der Aus- und Weiterbildung junger Menschen.

Siemens Linz could be termed the embodiment of the early vision that led to Industry 4.0. Here, the future is shaped: in the global Siemens headquarters for the development of highly complex automation for the automotive and aviation industries. And here there is every justification in speaking of "qualities with a pedigree": Siemens opened its first engineering offices in Linz in 1902. Today, Siemens Upper Austria also takes a leading role in training and further education for young people.

IMPULS-GEBER

DRIVING FORCE

Regional verankert, gerne an vorderster Front und wirtschaftlich weltoffen aufgestellt. Die Raiffeisenlandesbank OÖ, mit ihrer Zentrale am Südbahnhofmarkt, wurde 1900 als Spitzeninstitut der Raiffeisenbankengruppe OÖ gegründet. Mit einem umfassenden Netzwerk, mehr als 350 Beteiligungen und neun Standorten in Süddeutschland ist der Konzern für Privatkunden in der Region ebenso gerüstet wie für „big finance".

Rooted in the region, often breaking new ground, focused on the global economy. The Raiffeisen Landesbank Upper Austria, with its head offices at the Südbahnhofmarkt, was founded in 1900 as the central institution of the Raiffeisen group of banks in the province. With an extensive network, more than 350 holdings and nine branches in southern Germany the concern serves private customers in the region as well as "big finance".

BODENVEREDLER

PLOTTING IMPROVEMENTS

Den Wert von Boden und Immobilien weiß man im Wachstumswunder Linz zu schätzen. „Mit Blick aufs Ganze" bringt die Bau und Boden Immobiliengruppe seit 50 Jahren Wohn- und Nutzwerte vor allem in Linz und Oberösterreich zum Wachsen. Die Palette reicht von kleinen, feinen Lagen bis zu innovativen Wohnkonzepten in der städtischen Quartiersentwicklung.

Real estate is highly valued in Linz, a city where growth is phenomenal. The real estate developers Bau und Boden have been enhancing the value of residential and commercial sites for fifty years, chiefly in Linz and Upper Austria and always with their eyes on "the big picture". Their portfolio ranges from small but sought-after sites to innovative concepts for urban housing developments.

DAS NEUE UND DAS KÜHNE

THE NEW AND THE BOLD

2.2

Scharenweise parken vor den Eingängen der einstigen Tabakfabrik Fahrräder und E-Scooter. Turmhoch und ein historisches Relikt der Schlot bei der Maschinenhalle, aus der das Wummern der Gebäudetechnik dringt. Als kreatives Brummen setzt es sich fort bis in die letzten Winkel des Areals.

Cycles and e-scooters throng the entrances to the Tabakfabrik, the former tobacco factory. The chimney by the machine hall is as tall as a tower and a relic of history. From it, the hum of the building's plant can be heard; it penetrates every nook and cranny of the site as a creative buzz.

Wo noch 2009 Tausende Arbeiter Zigarettentabak fertigten, weisen heute Schilder den Weg zur „start-up mall", zum „cloud-fight" oder zum Valie-Export-Center mit einer Werkschau der gleichnamigen Linzer Kunstikone Valie Export. In der „Grand Garage" stehen für Interessierte Basics im Schweißen und 3-D-Druck auf dem Programm oder „Lasercut für Kids". Über tausend Kreative und Tüftler haben mittlerweile im freien Ideen- und Veranstaltungsraum der Tabakfabrik ihre Jobs gefunden oder selbst geschaffen. Die Stadt ist daran ebenso aktiv beteiligt wie nur wenige Hundert Meter entfernt am TECHCENTER Winterhafen, einem weiteren „schnellen Brüter" für junge Unternehmen.

Linz sieht in Linz die innovativste Stadt Österreichs. Und man glaubt es der „UNESCO City of Media Art" aufs Wort. In keiner anderen Stadt kommen auf gut 200.000 Einwohner so viele Patente. Manche so kühn, dass sie die Welt verändern könnten. So tastet sich die voestalpine am Standort bereits an eine Stahlerzeugung heran, die nicht auf Koks, sondern auf erneuerbarer Energie und Wasserstoff basiert.

Auf dem Weg von der Stahlstadt zur nach wie vor industriell geprägten Digitalstadt hat Linz die Zielgerade erreicht. Künstliche Intelligenz kokettiert mit der Kunst, das Internet der Dinge wird zur Sache der Bürger. So wie am „Innovationshauptplatz" der Stadt, wo jede und jeder eingeladen ist, mit neuen Ideen die Zukunft der Stadt mitzugestalten. Aus der reinen Freude am Fortschritt – und bei Eignung auch als Business Case. Ein Platz in der Tabakfabrik wird sich finden.

Where thousands of workers were still making cigarette tobacco in 2009, signs now point to the "start-up mall", the "cloud-fight" and the Valie Export centre with an exhibition of works by the iconic artist and native of Linz Valie Export. The "Grand Garage" offers basic welding and 3D printing for those interested, as well as laser-cutting for kids. Over one thousand creatives and innovators have now found, or created, their jobs at the Tabakfabrik, the free space for ideas and events. The city government is just as actively involved here as it is in the TECHCENTER Winterhafen a few hundred metres away, another "rapid incubator" for young companies.

Linz sees Linz as Austria's most innovative city. And what the "UNESCO City of Media Art" says of itself is entirely believable. In no other town are so many patents issued per 200,000 inhabitants. And some are so bold that they could change the world. For instance, voestalpine is exploring a method of steel-making based not on coke but on renewable forms of energy and hydrogen.

Linz now has the finish line in its sights as it evolves from a city of steel to a digital city still defined by industry. Artificial intelligence flirts with art, the Internet of Things becomes a matter for the people. Just like at the city's "innovation hub" where everyone is invited to help shape the city's future with new ideas. Purely for the joy of progress – and if suitable, as a business case too. There will always be room at the Tabakfabrik.

IDEENFABRIK
IDEA FACTORY

Rauchende Köpfe statt rauchender Kunden bringen seit 2009 Leben in das denkmalgeschützte Architekturjuwel der Tabakfabrik. An die 2.000 Kreative aus Bereichen wie der Kreativwirtschaft, Soziales, Handwerk, Bildung oder Start-ups schaffen die Jobs und Perspektiven der Zukunft.

Since 2009 bright sparks have filled the Tabakfabrik with life – this architectural gem and listed building where the only sparks were once those from customers' cigarettes. Around 2,000 creatives from fields including the creative industry, social affairs, crafts, education and start-ups are creating the jobs and perspectives of the future.

MULTI-MEDIA

WAS DAS HERZ BEGEHRT

HEART'S DESIRES

Shoppen & Genießen über alle Branchen ist das süße, tägliche Brot in der LentiaCity: von Mode über Kosmetik bis Schmuck. Vom Restaurant bis zur Vinothek. Seit der Neueröffnung 2010 erstrahlt die Shopping-Welt im Herzen Urfahrs in neuem Glanz und exotischen Facetten.

Shops and treats of every kind are the tempting stock-in-trade of LentiaCity: from fashion to cosmetics to jewellery. From restaurants to wine shops. The shopping Mecca in the heart of the Urfahr district was reopened in 2010 with a stunning new look and exotic touches.

Fab
AR
efin
INGENIEU
P
Parkscheine

FABAHAFT

FABALOUS

Fabasoft zählt seit der Gründung 1988 zu den Vorreitern und heute zu den Stars innovativer Software-Entwicklung am Standort Linz. Weit über Europa hinaus gestalten renommierte Konzerne und öffentliche Verwaltungen mithilfe von Fabasoft-Produkten digitale Prozesse, die höchsten Ansprüchen an Effizienz und Sicherheit gerecht werden.

Fabasoft, founded in Linz in 1988 as a pioneer of innovative software development, now ranks among the leading lights in the sector. Prominent companies and government bodies far beyond the borders of Europe use Fabasoft products to develop digital processes that meet the very highest standards of efficiency and security.

GRENZERFAHRUNG

BORDERLINE EXPERIENCES

Das Ars Electronica Center macht digitale Technologien zum Gegenstand wie zum Mittel der Erfahrung. Maßgeblich hat es das Profil des modernen Linz als Experimentierraum zwischen Gesellschaft, Technologie und Kunst mitgeprägt. Eine Führung durch das Haus erweitert den Horizont: bisweilen spielerisch, dann wieder mit geballter digitaler Power wie im *Space 8K*, wo eine interstellare Reise zur dreidimensionalen Grenzerfahrung wird.

The Ars Electronica Center makes digital technologies both the object and the means of discovery. It has been instrumental in shaping the modern identity of Linz as a site of experimentation between society, technology and art. A tour of the building broadens the visitor's horizons: sometimes playfully, and then with the full force of digital power, for example in Space 8K in which an interstellar journey becomes a three-dimensional exploration of limits.

WOLKENDESIGN

CLOUD DESIGN

Stahlstadt wird Digitalstadt. Auch wenn das Headquarter von Dynatrace heute nahe Boston in den USA liegt, Gründungsort und Herz der Software-Entwicklung ist Linz. Auf Basis von Cloud-Technologie und künstlicher Intelligenz entwickelt das Unternehmen neue Qualitäten in der Automatisierung und in der digitalen Erfahrung für Anwender in Industrie, Dienstleistung, Finanzsektor oder öffentlicher Verwaltung.

From steel city to digital city. Although the headquarters of Dynatrace are now located near Boston, USA, its origins, and the heart of its software development, are in Linz. Using cloud technology and artificial intelligence the company creates new qualities of automation and digital interaction for practitioners in industry, the service branch, the financial sector and government bodies.

HÖCHSTPERSÖNLICH

HIGHLY PERSONAL

Im Neuen Rathaus auf der Urfahraner Seite der Innenstadt öffnet schon morgens um sieben das BürgerInnen-Service der Stadt. Hier werden Wohnsitze umgemeldet, Reisedokumente ausgestellt oder Aktivpässe mit vielen Vergünstigungen für Linzer mit geringerem Einkommen vergeben. Vieles geht in der Verwaltung schon digital – bis hin zur Plattform „Schau auf Linz“: Ein loser Kanaldeckel oder ein defekter Fahrkartenautomat wird damit kurzerhand per App an die Stadtverwaltung gemeldet ...

In the New Town Hall on the Urfahr (northern) side of the city centre the one-stop offices for citizens' administrative affairs open at 7 a.m. Here, changes of address are recorded, travel documents issued, and the Linz "Aktivpass" can be collected which grants price reductions on many services to lower-income citizens. Many administrative tasks have already been digitised, including the "Schau auf Linz" ("Look after Linz") platform: With this app, a loose manhole cover or broken ticket machine can be reported to the authorities without delay...

mic

REIBUNGSLOS
FRICTIONLESS

Grenzen überwinden erleichtert das 1988 in Linz gegründete Unternehmen MIC mit Software: Integrierte Zolllösungen machen den reibungslosen globalen Warenverkehr kosteneffizienter, transparenter und sicherer. Und MIC zu einem Global Player: Die ausgereiften Lösungen der Linzer Software-Schmiede stehen weltweit im Einsatz.

The company MIC, founded in Linz in 1988, provides software that facilitates frictionless border crossings: integrated customs solutions make the movement of goods more cost-effective, efficient, easier to track and safer throughout the world – and MIC a global player: the market-ready solutions from the Linz software developers are deployed worldwide.

DAS FLIESSEN UND DAS GLEITEN

THE FLOW AND THE GLIDE

2.3

Unbewegt stehen vor der Pfarrkirche zu St. Magdalena nur die alten Kastanien. Fuß- und Radwanderer promenieren auf der Trasse der historischen Pferdeeisenbahn vorbei. Weit unten, im Weichbild der Stadt, strömt die Donau, blitzen Pylone von Brücken, streben und kurven mächtige Verkehrswege nach allen Richtungen.

The only things not moving by St. Magdalena's church are the old chestnut trees in front of it. Hikers and cyclists promenade along the route once travelled by the historical horse-drawn railway. Far below, in the city precincts, the Danube flows, bridge pylons flash, and broad thoroughfares stretch and weave every which way.

Internat. Linien
Park-deck
Bahnhofsvorplatz
Ausgang exit
POLIZEI
BITTE STIEGE FREI
HALTEN

ERINNERUNGSTAFEL PFERDEEISENBAHN ANNO 1832 1872
GMUNDEN-LINZ-ST·MAGDALENA-BUDWEIS

Wann immer es schneller und weiter gehen musste, hat Linz dem Fortschritt einen Weg gebahnt. 1832 gleich mit einer Weltneuheit: Die Pferdeeisenbahn läutete als der „erste Schienenverkehr des öffentlichen Verkehrs auf dem Festlande in Europa" eine neue Zeit ein. Von Pferden gezogen und auf Schienen gleitend, erreichte so das Salz aus Gmunden das böhmische Budweis über Linz in wenigen Tagen. Ebenso wie gut und gerne 150.000 Reisende jedes Jahr.

Salz spielt heute am kraftstrotzenden Wirtschaftsstandort Linz keine Hauptrolle mehr. Rohstoffe, Betriebsmittel, Komponenten und Waren wollen umgeschlagen werden. Täglich ein Heer an Pendlern sucht den zügigen Weg durch jene Stadt, die jeden vierten Arbeitsplatz in Oberösterreich beherbergt. Linz hat dazu alle Register eines modernen und innovativen Verkehrswesens gezogen. Den „Ur-Motor" der Donau mit einem Handels- und einem Tankhafen zusätzlich produktiv gemacht. Mit der Mühlkreisautobahn über Brücken und durch Tunnels den Anschluss an die nationale Hauptschlagader der Westautobahn und zum nahen Airport Linz geschaffen. Und an den Gleisen der Westbahn Highspeed mit Service verbunden mit einer Verkehrsdrehscheibe, die regelmäßig zum „schönsten Bahnhof Österreichs" gewählt wird.

„Imovation" schreiben sich Forscher und Entscheider in Linz weiterhin auf ihre Fahnen. Mit Global Playern in der E-Mobilität kooperieren sie ebenso wie mit einem chinesischen Konsortium bei der Entwicklung und Testung unbemannter Flugtaxis. Oben bei der alten Pferdeeisenbahn wird der beste Platz sein, um sie fliegen zu sehen.

Whenever it was necessary to go faster and further, Linz paved the way for progress. And did so in 1832 with a world first: the horse-drawn railway, the "first rail-bound public transport in mainland Europe", heralded the dawn of a new era. Pulled by horses and gliding on rails, salt from Gmunden reached Budějovice in Bohemia via Linz in a matter of days. As did at least 150,000 travellers every year.

Salt no longer plays a significant role in the thriving centre of commerce and industry that is Linz. Instead, raw materials, equipment, parts and merchandise are handled here. Every day, hordes of commuters seek the fastest way across the city where every fourth job in Upper Austria is located. To this end, Linz has pulled out all the stops to provide a modern and innovative transport network. Has enhanced the productivity of the Danube, the "original motor", with a trade port and tanker port. Has linked the Mühlkreis-Autobahn to the Westautobahn, Austria's main artery, over bridges and through tunnels, and to the nearby Linz Airport. And has combined high speed and service on the tracks of the Western Railway with a transport hub which is regularly voted "Austria's most attractive railway station".

Researchers and decision-makers in Linz continue to embrace "imovation". They are collaborating with global players in the e-mobility sector and a Chinese consortium on developing and trialling pilotless air taxis. And the best place to watch them flying will be up by the old horse-drawn railway line.

STROMGEWALT

RIVER POWER

Tuche, Häute und Salz kamen einst auf der Donau und etablierten Linz schon in der frühen Neuzeit als notablen Handelsstandort. Ab 1842 verließen die ersten Eisenschiffe des Kontinentes die Linzer Schiffswerft. Heute profitieren Industrie und Handel in Linz vom umschlagstärksten Hafen an der oberen Donau.

Cloth, skins and salt were once carried on the Danube and established Linz as a significant centre of trade at the beginning of the modern age. In 1842 the continent's first iron ships left the Linz shipyard. Today, industry and trade in Linz profit from the port with the greatest volume of goods on the Upper Danube.

LINZ AG HAFEN
CMA CGM
CMA CGM

DER WELT VERBUNDEN

GLOBAL CONNECTIONS

Die Hafenstadt Linz beherbergt mit dem „Mural Harbor" eine der größten Graffiti-Galerien der Welt. Mit dem öffentlichen Hafen und dem voestalpine-Werkshafen vor allem auch den bedeutendsten Umschlagplatz an der oberen Donau. Rund um die besucherfreundliche Hafendirektion erstrecken sich Containerterminal, Handels- und Tankhafen mit modernen Umschlaganlagen zwischen Lagerhäusern und Speziallagern für Tiefkühl- und Gefahrgut.

Linz, the city of ports, is home to one of the world's biggest graffiti galleries: the "Mural Harbor". And, with the public port and the voestalpine works docks, to the Upper Danube's most important port of trans-shipment as well. The docks administrative offices, which can be visited, are surrounded by the container terminal, trade port and tanker port with modern trans-shipment plant between warehouses and special storage facilities for frozen goods and hazardous materials.

ARTERIE

ARTERY

Die Nibelungenbrücke setzt gleich nach dem Linzer Hauptplatz zum eleganten Schwung über die Donau an. Eine Brücke existiert an dieser Stelle hinüber nach Urfahr schon seit einem halben Jahrtausend. Oft in der Geschichte bildete sie eine Grenze, heute ist sie eine zentrale Arterie im gemeinsamen „Blutkreislauf" der Stadt.

The Nibelungenbrücke begins its elegant sweep across the Danube immediately after the main square in Linz. A bridge to Urfahr on the northern bank has existed on this site for half a millennium. Often a border in earlier days, it is now a key artery in the city's integral "circulation".

BRAND AUS

FIRE PROOF

Gegründet 1866 als Handelshaus für Feuerwehrbedarf in Linz, ist Rosenbauer heute der weltweit führende Systemanbieter für Brand- und Katastrophenschutz. Vom Stiefel über Schneidlöschsysteme bis hin zum Flughafenlöschfahrzeug: Wo Rosenbauer draufsteht, ist Hightech drin und höchste Sicherheit für die Einsatzkräfte garantiert. Linz ist aber nicht nur der Sitz der Konzernzentrale, hier werden jährlich auch um die 150.000 Feuerwehrhelme für den Weltmarkt montiert.

Founded in Linz in 1866 as a trader in fire-fighting equipment, Rosenbauer is now the world's leading supplier of fire protection and disaster control systems. From boots to cutting extinguishing systems to airport fire engines: the name of Rosenbauer guarantees high-tech and maximum safety for the emergency services. But Linz is not just where the concern is headquartered: it is also where around 150,000 fire-fighters' helmets are produced every year for the global market.

FELBERMAYR

ZU NEUEM UFER

TO NEW SHORES

„Entspannung unterwegs" signalisiert diese Baustelle gestressten Pendlern. 400 Meter lang, bringt die „Neue Donaubrücke" frischen Verkehrsfluss über dem Fluss – für Autos ebenso wie für Radfahrer und Fußgänger. Und das als Ausdruck dezidierten Bürgerwillens: In einer Volksbefragung 2015 waren es die Linzer, die für eine Demontage der alten Eisenbahn- und den Bau der neuen Donaubrücke gestimmt haben.

"Relief is on its way" is the message this building project has for stressed-out commuters. The 400-metre "new Danube bridge" will improve traffic flow across the river – not just for motorists but for cyclists and pedestrians too. And that as the result of express public opinion: in a poll in 2015, it was the population of Linz itself that voted to demolish the old railway bridge and build the new road bridge.

EINGANG
InfoPoint
Lass dich nicht aus der Bahn werfen.
ÖBB
SPAR
Tickets

REISEFERTIG

READY TO DEPART

Das Kommen und Gehen ist auf dem Linzer Hauptbahnhof im Minutentakt organisiert und von Shops und Gastronomie gründlich serviciert. Von hier geht es nach überallhin: mit der 10.000 PS starken Taurus-Lok der ÖBB in kaum eineinhalb Stunden nach Wien, mit der Linzer Lokalbahn ins Umland, per Bus oder Bim in die Stadt. Die markanten „Linzer Löwen" am Eingang waren übrigens für Salzburg bestimmt, um dann in Linz nach den Wirren des Zweiten Weltkriegs ihre neue Heimat zu finden.

The comings and goings at Linz central station are organised to the minute and all other wishes met by the shops and restaurants there. From here you can go anywhere: to Vienna in barely 90 minutes with the Austrian Railways' 10,000-horsepower Taurus locomotive; to the surrounding area on the local railway; into the city on buses and trams. By the way, the distinctive "Linz lions" at the station entrance were originally intended for Salzburg but ended up in Linz following the turmoil of World War II.

AUF SICHEREM GLEIS

SAFELY ON TRACK

Hochleistungstechnologie von Plasser & Theurer erledigt heute mit maximaler Präzision, was in der Vergangenheit körperliche Schwerarbeit erfordert hat: den Bau und die Instandhaltung von Gleisen. Als Weltmarktführer liefert das Unternehmen Gleisbaumaschinen aus seinem Stammwerk in Linz in über 100 Länder weltweit.

High-performance technology by Plasser & Theurer now does jobs with perfect precision that once required heavy manual labour: the laying and maintenance of railway tracks. As the global market leader, the company supplies railway track machinery to over 100 countries worldwide from its headquarters in Linz.

BRÜCKENBAUER

BRIDGE BUILDERS

Ob Verkehrsströme oder die Realisierung des privaten Wohntraums: Die Linzer Swietelsky AG mit Niederlassungen und Töchtern in 19 Ländern baut Brücken vom Jetzt ins Morgen. Zwei „Bypass"-Konstruktionen entlang der Voestbrücke führen direkt in die Zukunft des Wirtschaftsstandortes Linz: Bis zu 100.000 Pendler täglich überqueren hier rasant die Donau.

For the flow of traffic or dream homes: the Linz firm of Swietelsky AG has offices and subsidiaries in nineteen countries and builds bridges leading to the future. Two "bypass" structures along the Voestbrücke form a direct route to the future of Linz as a centre of trade and industry: Every day, as many as 100,000 commuters speed across the Danube here.

ZUM BOARDING, BITTE!

ALL ABOARD!

180 Personen finden in den brandneuen Doppelgelenk-O-Bussen der LINZ AG LINIEN Platz. Ihre Bahnen ziehen die knapp 25 Meter langen Riesen rein elektrisch und damit emissionsfrei. Ausgestattet mit WLAN, verbinden sie die Beweglichkeit eines Busses mit der Effizienz der Straßenbahn. Die wiederum bildet mit vier Linien und der Pöstlingbergbahn die Grundlage für die engmaschige städtische Mobilität in Linz.

180 passengers fit into the brand-new bi-articulated trolleybuses operated by LINZ AG LINIEN. The almost 25-metre-long giants are powered entirely by electricity and are therefore emission-free. Equipped with Wi-Fi they combine the manoeuvrability of buses with the efficiency of trams. The latter, comprising four lines and the Pöstlingberg railway, complete the dense network of urban mobility in Linz.

LNZ

Ein Businessflug nach Frankfurt, die Reise in den Urlaub oder die Luftfracht nach Istanbul: Wo das LNZ-Kürzel auf dem Kofferschild oder auf den Frachtpapieren auftaucht, ist der Airport Linz im Spiel. Als zweitgrößter regionaler Frachtflughafen in Österreich mit angeschlossenem Wirtschaftspark wurde er zum Impulsgeber weit über den Raum Linz hinaus.

A business trip to Frankfurt, a holiday flight or freight transport to Istanbul: whenever the abbreviation LNZ appears on a luggage label or freight documents, Linz Airport is involved. As Austria's second-largest regional freight airport with an adjoining business park it has been a driving force of the economy in Linz and beyond.

GROSSES GESCHIEHT

GREAT THINGS ARE HAPPENING

3.456 Glaspaneele fluten Flure und Flächen mit Tageslicht: Das 1993 eröffnete Design Center fungierte als Taktgeber beim Aufstieg von Linz zur boomenden Kongressstadt. Neben Tagungen und Messen wie der viel besuchten WEIN & GENUSS weisen hier auch innovative Formate die Trends der Zukunft. Darunter CO_2-neutrale Green Meetings und virtuelle Konferenzen mit Teilnehmern aus aller Welt.

3,456 glass panels flood corridors and surfaces with daylight: the Design Center, opened in 1993, set the pace as Linz grew into a flourishing congress city. Besides conferences and trade fairs such as the hugely popular WEIN & GENUSS, innovative formats herald the trends of the future, such as carbon-neutral green meetings and virtual conferences with participants from all over the world.

RAUM FÜR MEHR

ROOM FOR MORE

Erste Adresse war der Adalbert-Stifter-Platz 2 nächst dem Linzer Hauptplatz schon in historischen Zeiten. Der Gasthof „Zum Erzherzog Karl" an dieser Stelle zählte seinerzeit zu den vornehmsten der Stadt. Seit dem Bau des Generali-Bürogebäudes 1962 laufen hier in der Regionaldirektion die Fäden zusammen, in der es um Versichern und Vorsorgen für alle Lebensbereiche geht. Das frei stehende Gebäude mit der streng gegliederten Fassade überrascht im Inneren mit Licht und Weite.

The first address, back in the mists of time, was Adalbert Stifter Platz 2 by Linz main square. In those days, the inn "Zum Erzherzog Karl" that stood on the site was one of the finest in the city. Since the Generali offices were built in 1962, the regional headquarters have served as the hub for all matters relating to insurance and providing for every eventuality. The stand-alone building with its sternly structured facade is surprisingly bright and spacious inside.

Grottenbahn
Zwergenreich & Märchenwelt
504

BAHNTRAUM

A DREAM ALL ALONG THE LINE

Steil geht es zu, wenn die Pöstlingbergbahn die Talfahrt hinunter zum Linzer Hauptplatz in Angriff nimmt. Nur in Lissabon findet man in Europa eine Adhäsionsbahn, die ähnliche Steigungsgrade bewältigt. Die Fahrt vorbei an verträumten Villen zwischen blühenden Wiesen und durch idyllische Haltestellen zieht jedes Jahr Hunderttausende Gäste an.

It's a sharp drop when the Pöstlingberg tram leaves the summit to go back down to Linz's main square. In Europe, only Lisbon has an adhesion railway system that can cope with similar gradients. The route, past dreamy villas between blooming meadows and with idyllic stops, attracts hundreds of thousands of passengers every year.

STADTDORF

CITY VILLAGE

St. Magdalena nördlich der Donau war bis 1938 eine eigene Gemeinde. Mit seiner Pfarrkirche hat sich der Ort etwas von seinem dörflichen Charme bewahrt. Eng angebunden an die Stadt Linz ist er schon seit historischen Zeiten: 1832 wurde hier in Anwesenheit von Kaiser Franz I. mit Pomp die „Erste Pferdeeisenbahn" von Gmunden nach Budweis eröffnet.

Until 1938, St. Magdalena north of the Danube was a village in its own right. With its parish church it has retained something of its rural charm. It has had close links with Linz for centuries: in 1832 the first-ever horse-drawn railway, from Gmunden to Budějovice, was opened with great ceremony in the presence of Emperor Franz I.

WIENER STÄDTISCHE

EINE WIENER IN LINZ
A VIENNESE IN LINZ

Sicherheit wurzelt in Beständigkeit: Bereits vor dem Ersten Weltkrieg hat die Wiener Städtische – heute führend insbesondere bei Lebensversicherungen – eine Generalrepräsentanz für Oberösterreich eingerichtet. Über ein Jahrhundert und mehrere Umzüge ging das Unternehmen mit der Stadt durch dick und dünn. Seit 2015 steht Kunden, Mitarbeitern und Partnern vis-à-vis des Brucknerhauses eine modern renovierte Landesdirektion zur Verfügung.

Security has its roots in stability: Wiener Städtische – now a leading insurer with a focus on life assurance – had already established an exclusive agency for Upper Austria before the First World War. In the course of a century, and relocating several times, the company went through thick and thin along with the city. Since 2015 modern, refurbished regional headquarters opposite the Brucknerhaus have welcomed customers, staff and partners.

VI

DAS SCHÖNE, DAS SCHICKE UND DAS SCHRÄGE.

AESTHETIC, ATTRACTIVE AND ALTERNATIVE.

WISSEN IST MACHEN

KNOWLEDGE IS DOING

3.1

Eine Gruppe Zehnjähriger lässt sich in 3-D und 8-K-Auflösung durch die Galaxien des „Deep Space" beamen. Eine halbe Stunde später und ein Stockwerk höher testen sie die Grenzen künstlicher Intelligenz aus. Um schließlich ihren Vormittag im AEC bei Musik zu beschließen, die nach Mozart klingt und vom Computer stammt.

A group of ten-year-olds is beamed through the galaxies of deep space in 3D and 8k resolution. Half an hour later and one floor higher they are testing the limits of artificial intelligence. And they end their morning at the AEC with music that sounds like Mozart and comes from the computer.

JKU
PARK

Einen Besuch im Linzer Ars Electronica Center vergisst man nicht. Das „Museum der Zukunft" wird zur höchst persönlichen und zur höchst lebendigen Begegnung mit den Möglichkeiten digitaler Technologien. Unabhängig von Alter und Geschlecht, triggert er bei Besuchern jenes technisch-naturwissenschaftliche „Erweckungserlebnis", von dem dann IT-, Biologie- oder Chemielehrer monatelang profitieren.

Überhaupt stellte sich die Bildungs- und Forschungsstadt Linz als in der Wolle gefärbte „Praktikerin" dar, bevor sie noch nach akademischen Würden strebte. Johannes Kepler hat in dieser Stadt vor vier Jahrhunderten sein astronomisches Hauptwerk vollendet, Josef Ressel als der spätere Erfinder der Schiffsschraube hier die Schule besucht. Hochschulstadt wurde Linz aber erst als boomender Wirtschaftsstandort 1966 mit der heutigen Johannes Kepler Universität. Den Uni-Campus an den grünen Hängen nahe dem Pöstlingberg lässt der „Science Park" wie eine futuristische Remise für Raumschiffe wirken. Gegliedert in kühne Gebäudetrakte, köchelt dort elektronische, mechatronische oder mikrosensorische Forschung in Zusammenarbeit mit dem Who's who der internationalen Industrie.

Als Ort der wissenschaftlichen Reflexion verstehen sich die Hochschulen in Linz wie etwa die Katholische Privatuniversität. Und es wäre nicht das moderne Linz, würde nicht Kunst die Technologie reflektieren und inspirieren: Vor allem die Linzer Kunsthochschule und die Bruckneruniversität für Musik, Schauspiel und Tanz haben sich internationalen Ruf erworben. Wer in Linz hoch hinauswill, beginnt aber am besten in der öffentlichen Bibliothek: Für sie hat die Stadt schon 2007 und 63 Meter hoch einen eigenen „Wissensturm" erbaut.

You don't forget a visit to the Ars Electronica Center in Linz. The "Museum of the Future" becomes a highly personal and highly dynamic encounter with the possibilities offered by digital technologies. In visitors of all ages and both sexes it triggers the "moment of awakening" to technology and science that teachers of IT, biology and chemistry benefit from for months to come.

As a city of education and research, Linz presents itself first and foremost as a dyed-in-the-wool practitioner, before it thought of striving for academic distinction. Four centuries ago, Johannes Kepler completed his magnum opus in astronomy here, and Josef Ressel, who went on to invent the marine propeller, went to school in the city. However, it was not until 1966 that Linz, a booming centre of trade and industry, became a university town with the foundation of what is now the Johannes Kepler University. The "Science Park" gives the university campus on the green slopes near the Pöstlingberg the look of a futuristic depot for spaceships. There, spread among the building's bold wings, electronic, mechatronic and micro-sensor research in association with the who's who of international industry simmers along.

Linz's universities, such as the Catholic Private University, see themselves as centres of scientific reflection. And it would not be modern-day Linz if art did not reflect and inspire technology: in particular, the University of Art and Design Linz and the Bruckner University of Music, Drama and Dance have earned an international reputation. Anyone desiring "higher" education would do well to start at the public library, where the city erected a 63-metre-high "knowledge tower" in 2007.

EXZELLENZ IN PROGRESS

EXCELLENCE IN PROGRESS

Technologien und Ideen von morgen stehen täglich im Mittelpunkt der Arbeit an der Johannes Kepler Universität Linz. Dazu die optimale Vorbereitung von über 20.000 Studierenden auf die Anforderungen des modernen Arbeitsmarktes. Als eine der größten Arbeitgeberinnen und als größte Bildungseinrichtung bildet die JKU eine Säule des Wirtschaftsstandorts Oberösterreich. Technologie und Ökonomie finden hier ebenso zu Exzellenz wie Recht und Medizin, Sozial-, Kultur- und Naturwissenschaften.

Tomorrow's technologies and ideas are the focus of the work done every day at the Johannes Kepler University, Linz. Along with giving 20,000 students exactly what they need to meet the requirements of today's job market. The JKU is one of Upper Austria's biggest employers and educational institutions and as such a pillar of the region as a centre of commerce and industry. Here, excellence is achieved in technology and economics, but also in law and medicine, the sciences, social sciences and cultural studies.

KULTUR-KONTUR
CULTURAL CONTOURS

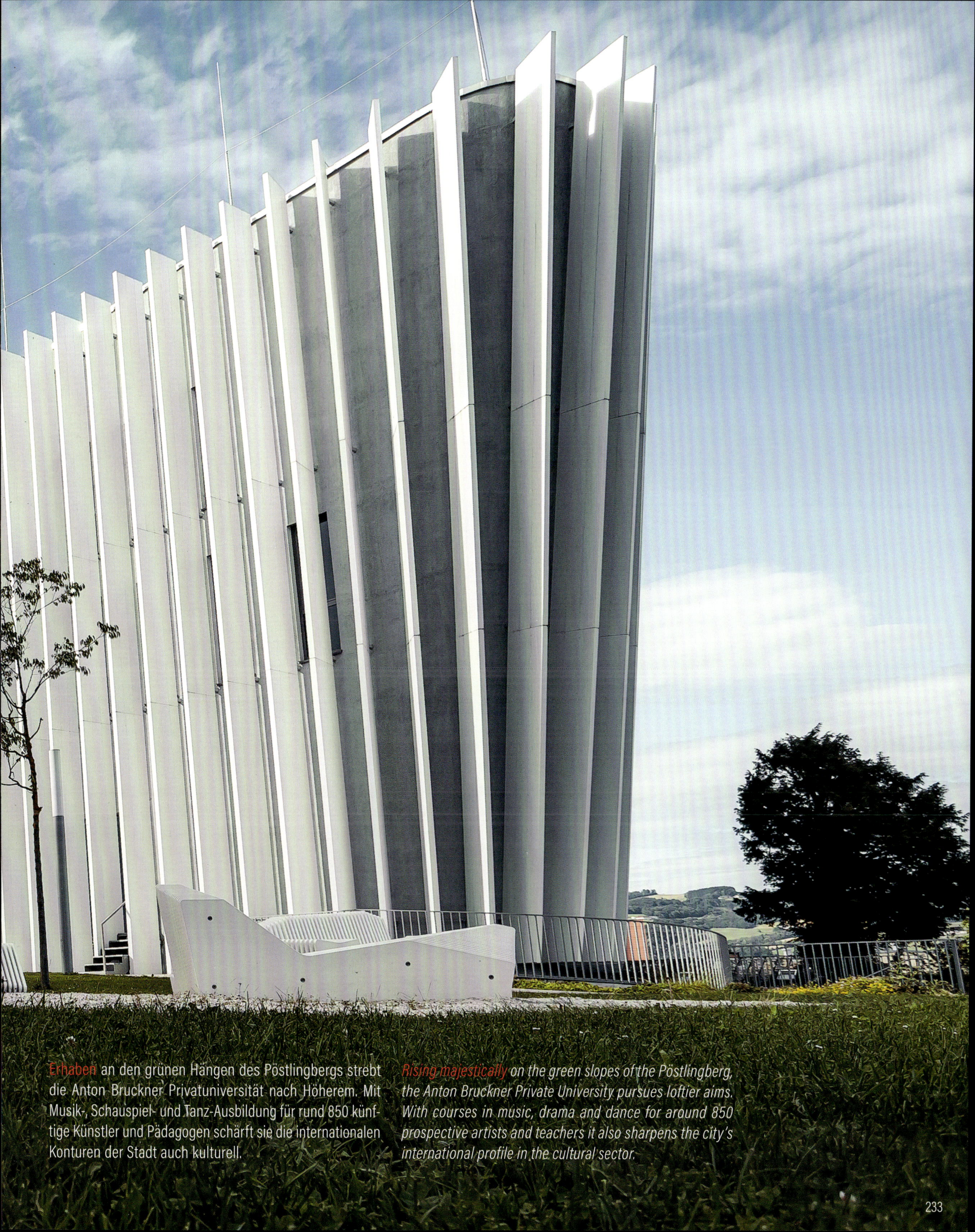

Erhaben an den grünen Hängen des Pöstlingbergs strebt die Anton Bruckner Privatuniversität nach Höherem. Mit Musik-, Schauspiel- und Tanz-Ausbildung für rund 850 künftige Künstler und Pädagogen schärft sie die internationalen Konturen der Stadt auch kulturell.

Rising majestically on the green slopes of the Pöstlingberg, the Anton Bruckner Private University pursues loftier aims. With courses in music, drama and dance for around 850 prospective artists and teachers it also sharpens the city's international profile in the cultural sector.

BILDUNGSBURG

BASTION OF EDUCATION

Die Sternwarte im Zentrum des Gebäudes wirkt für die Schüler des Petrinums wie Ansporn und Mahnung, den Sinn nach Höherem zu richten. Seit über 120 Jahren bildet das Bischöfliche Gymnasium am Fuße des Pöstlingbergs eine feste Institution in der Linzer Bildungslandschaft.

The observatory at the centre of the building serves the pupils of the Petrinum as an incentive and a reminder to turn their minds to loftier concerns. The episcopal Gymnasium at the foot of the Pöstlingberg has occupied a firm place among Linz's educational institutions for over 120 years.

BILDUNGSWERTE

EDUCATIONAL VALUES

Zauberhaft fast wie Harry Potters Hogwarts-Schule mutet das Kollegium Aloisianum an. Hinter der romantischen Fassade auf dem Freinberg herrscht der bildungsbeflissene Alltag eines privaten katholischen Gymnasiums mit Öffentlichkeitsrecht. Die seit 1912 bestehende Schule bekennt sich zu einer Erziehung nach jesuitischen Prinzipien.

The Kollegium Aloisianum (Aloysian College) appears almost as magical as Harry Potter's Hogwarts School. Behind the romantic facade of this private Catholic Gymnasium with state school rights, pupils attend their daily lessons, eager for knowledge. The school has been open since 1912 and provides education according to Jesuit principles.

HÖHERES WISSEN

HIGHER EDUCATION

Bildungsideale werden in Linz hochgehalten, und das im Sinne des Wortes: Im 63 Meter hohen „Wissensturm" im Volksgartenviertel genießen Kunden der Stadtbibliothek und der Volkshochschule eine wahrlich privilegierte Position. Veranstaltungen für die Jüngeren – vom KiWi-Lesefest bis zu den Jugendbuchtagen – würzen das Lesen und Lernen mit einem kräftigen Schuss Freude.

Educational objectives have high priority in Linz. Literally: in the 63-metre-high "knowledge tower" in the Volksgarten district, visitors to the municipal library and the adult education centre are in a truly privileged position. Events for youngsters, such as the KiWi reading festival or the young people's book days, add a generous portion of fun to reading and learning.

GERADLINIG

ON THE LEVEL

Qualität und Objektivität gelten als die höchsten Gebote bei KPMG. Der Linzer Standort, mit mittlerweile rund 450 Mitarbeitern, repräsentiert seit 75 Jahren das Know-how einer weltweit agierenden „Big Four"-Gesellschaft in der Wirtschaftsprüfung und Beratung. Und damit genau das, was den Ansprüchen der international orientierten Linzer Wirtschaft gerecht wird.

At KPMG, quality and objectivity are the watchwords. The Linz offices, which now have a workforce of around 450, have represented the expertise of a globally operating "big four" company in the auditing and consultancy sector for 75 years. And this is precisely what is required by the international aspirations of business and industry in Linz.

KUNST IST SPÜREN

ART IS FEELING

3.2

Hoch über dem Ursulinenhof lockt der „Höhenrausch" auf einen inspirierenden Holzweg. Unten mischen sich Bewohner der Stadt mit Kulturtouristen. Schwere Kost gibt's heute im Programmkino, leichte in der bunt gefächerten Gastro. Gerade ist die Tagung des regionalen Kulturvereins im Erdgeschoß zu Ende gegangen.

High above the Ursulinenhof, "Höhenrausch" entices those with a good head for heights onto an inspirational wooden path. Down below, citizens mingle with culture tourists. Today's films at the repertory cinema are heavy going, but the motley collection of cafés and restaurants offers lighter fare. The conference of the regional cultural association on the ground floor has just ended.

OTIS HISTORY
EXTENDED ELEVATOR

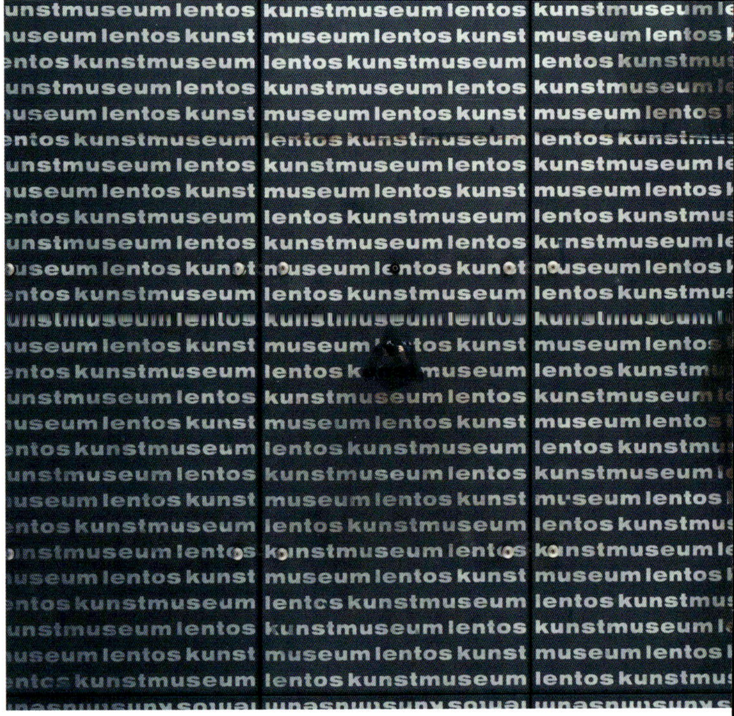
kunstmuseum lentos
museum lentos kunst
lentos kunstmuseum

Er kann als Urzelle in der Erfolgsgeschichte der jungen Kulturmacht Linz gelten: der Ursulinenhof mit dem heutigen „OÖ Kulturquartier". Viel verrät er über den Zugang der Linzer zu Kunst und Kultur: Es sind die Stärkung und Servicierung regionaler Initiativen, aus der am Ende eine weltoffene Szene von Rang erwächst.

Ein kulturelles Fundament für die Ewigkeit haben mit dem Komponisten Anton Bruckner und dem Schriftsteller Adalbert Stifter bereits zwei Leitgrößen des 19. Jahrhunderts bereitet. Und dabei schon jene produktive Spannung abgebildet, die Linz innewohnt: Irritierte Bruckner als progressiver Erneuerer viele seiner Zeitgenossen, liegt Stifter in seiner an Sturheit grenzenden Bedächtigkeit wie ein böhmischer Fels quer im reißenden Fahrwasser dieser Stadt. Vielleicht liebt und pflegt sie ihn gerade deswegen.

Die Eröffnung des Brucknerhauses als Konzertstätte bedeutete 1974 so etwas wie den „Urknall" für die internationale Kulturdestination Linz. Weitere folgten: Seit 1979 zieht die „Linzer Klangwolke" jeden September Zehntausende an. 2003 komplettierte das Lentos als Haus für zeitgenössische Kunst die „Kulturmeile" an der Donau. Und dann erst 2009: Als „Kulturhauptstadt Europas" präsentierte sich Linz auf großer Bühne. Der Neubau des Ars Electronica Centers verband das kulturelle Profil der Stadt endgültig mit ihrem innovativ-technologischen. Heute spiegelt der Kulturbetrieb Linzer Vielfalt und Vitalität wider: vom 2013 eröffneten Musiktheater über das Pop Sommer Open Air als Publikumsmagnet bis zur Straßenkunst des „Pflasterspektakels" und zum traditionsreichen Urfahraner Markt.

It can be seen as the cradle of Linz's success story as a young cultural power: the Ursulinenhof with the "OÖ Kulturquartier" it now houses. It says a lot about how the people of Linz approach art and culture: it is the promotion and servicing of regional initiatives that ultimately brings forth a cosmopolitan scene of repute.

Two leading lights from the nineteenth century, the composer Anton Bruckner and writer Adalbert Stifter, laid a cultural foundation for the ages. In the process they reflected the productive friction that is intrinsic to Linz: whereas Bruckner irritated many of his contemporaries as a progressive reformer, Stifter, with a deliberateness bordering on the stubborn, lies like a Bohemian rock across the raging torrent of this city. Perhaps this is why it loves him and cultivates him.

The opening of the Brucknerhaus as a concert venue in 1974 was something akin to the "big bang" for Linz as an international cultural centre. Others followed: since 1979, the "Linzer Klangwolke" has attracted tens of thousands every September. In 2003, Lentos completed the "cultural mile" on the Danube as a home of contemporary art. And then came 2009: as a "European Capital of Culture" Linz was able to present itself on a large stage. The reconstruction of the Ars Electronica Center finally combined the city's cultural identity with its profile as a centre of innovative technology. Today, cultural life in Linz reflects the city's diversity and vitality: from the Musiktheater that opened in 2013 to the crowd-pulling Pop Sommer Open Air to the street art of the "Pflasterspektakel" and the rich tradition of the Urfahraner Markt.

KULTURMEILE

CULTURAL MILE

Mit dem Lentos im Zentrum, flankiert von Brucknerhaus und Ars Electronica, vibriert die Linzer „Kulturmeile". Entlang beider Seiten der Donau verbindet sie Stadtteile, Lebenswelten und Visionen. 2009 ist Linz die „Kulturhauptstadt Europas" gewesen – und eine Kulturdestination von internationalem Rang geblieben.

With the Lentos Museum flanked by the Brucknerhaus and the Ars Electronica Center, the Linz "cultural mile" pulses with life. Along both sides of the Danube it connects districts, communities and visions. In 2009 Linz was "European Capital of Culture" – and has remained a cultural centre of international standing ever since.

GROSSE OPER
GRAND OPERA

Einen Vorhang symbolisiert die Fassade des 2013 eröffneten Musiktheaters beim Volksgarten. Ein Vorhang, der hier für Opern und Operetten ebenso aufgeht wie für zeitgemäß inszeniertes und junges Theater. Das Haus zählt zu den modernsten Opernhäusern Mitteleuropas. Es wäre nicht Linz, wäre nicht auch eine technologische Finesse im Spiel: Die Besucherplätze sind mit Touchscreens für die Anzeige übersetzter Sing- bzw. Sprechtexte ausgestattet.

The facade of the Musiktheater, located near the Volksgarten and opened in 2013, represents a curtain. A curtain that rises for operas and operettas as well as for contemporary theatre productions and theatre by young people. The Musiktheater is one of the most modern opera houses in central Europe. But it would not be Linz without a certain technological finesse: the seats in the auditorium are fitted with touchscreens that display translations of libretti or dialogues.

KUNST AM PULS DER ZEIT

ART FOR OUR TIMES

Ausstellungsansicht „Jakob Lena Knebl. Frau 49 Jahre alt“, Lentos Kunstmuseum Linz, 2020

Die Avantgarde schafft sich im Lentos auf 8.000 Quadratmeter Fläche facettenreich Ausdruck. Bestände von Klimt und Kokoschka über Valie Export bis hin zu Pop-Art und Street-Art haben das Haus international zum Fixpunkt unter den Museen für moderne und zeitgenössische Kunst geadelt.

At Lentos, the avant-garde is expressed in many different ways on 8,000 m². Collections ranging from Klimt and Kokoschka to Valie Export, along with works of pop art and street art, have established the museum as an international mainstay of modern and contemporary art.

Ausstellungsansicht „Josef Bauer. Demonstration“, Lentos Kunstmuseum Linz, 2020

AKUSTIK-WUNDER

AN ACOUSTIC MIRACLE

Symphonische Qualitäten beweist das Brucknerhaus akustisch wie architektonisch. 1974 mit Herbert von Karajan und den Wiener Philharmonikern eröffnet, geriet es zum gefeierten Debüt der internationalen Kulturstadt Linz und zum Grundstein der heutigen „Kulturmeile" an der Donau.

Symphonic qualities mark both the acoustics and the architecture of the Brucknerhaus. Opened in 1974 with Herbert von Karajan and the Vienna Philharmonic, it became the celebrated springboard of Linz as an international city of culture and the cornerstone of today's "cultural mile" on the Danube.

LEBEN IST BEWEGEN

LIVING IS MOVING

3.3

Drüben in der KAPU probt am frühen Abend schon der Hardcore-Punk. Drunten im Aquarium erklären für heute die ersten Studenten das Bier zur Kunst – oder auch umgekehrt. Platz ist in Linz für alle: Im Thüsen Tak, wo der Rock 'n' Roll gerade nachtaktiv wird, teilt man sich das Haus mit einem Hundesalon.

Over in the KAPU, hardcore punk rehearsals are already under way in the early evening. Down in the aquarium, this evening's first students are declaring that beer is art – or vice versa. Linz has room for everybody: Thüsen Tak, where rock 'n' roll is getting ready for its nightly activities, shares its home with a dog parlour.

Deep Purple
CLASSIC ROCK LEGENDS
Hard Rock
LINZ
CCCP
КУРЕНИЕ УБИВАЕТ

Gewachsene und lebendige Milieus sind es, die nicht nur die freie Szene in Linz zur bunten Szenerie runden: Die samstägliche Frühstücksschickeria auf der Donauterrasse des Lentos trägt ebenso ihre Farben bei wie die Hundertschaften von Flanierenden und Studierenden, die jeden Abend die Altstadt ziemlich jung aussehen lassen.

Inkludiert ist ein kräftiger Schuss jener Wildheit und Avantgarde, ohne die es sie nicht gibt: die urbane Lebensfreude. Die Stadtwerkstatt werkt als ältestes autonomes Kulturzentrum der Stadt schon seit 1979. Die KAPU, einer Jugendorganisation entwachsen, brachte schon ab den 1980ern den Punk nach Linz, den Hardcore aus Washington und den Hip-Hop aus New York. Im Thüsen Tak läutete Frank Zappa ebenso die Glocken der Moderne wie Deep-Purple-Mitbegründer Nick Simper. Neben englischen Szenebands war es Kurt Cobain, der Linz fix auf den Tourneeplan nahm. David Bowie spielte hier vor 30.000 Menschen.

Das Aufregende hat sich in dieser Stadt seine Kompromisslosigkeit bewahrt: setzt beim Crossing Europe Filmfestival mit engagiertem, zeitgenössischem Filmschaffen Akzente. Bringt im Stream Festival Pop und Digitalisierung auf einen elektrisierenden Nenner. Lässt im Posthof „zeitkultur am hafen" von der Leine und schafft im Mural Harbor die Freiheit und den Freiraum für die vermutlich größte Graffiti-Galerie Europas. Oder im Theater Phönix: Dort finden sich Klassiker entstaubt und junge Autoren auf der Bühne. Das Zitat des großen Linzers Anton Bruckner würden die Performer, Autoren und Regisseure der Linzer Gegenwartsszene wohl vorbehaltlos unterschreiben: Großes habe er fertiggebracht, „weil ich von Jugend an Ehrfurcht gehabt habe vor allem Echten und Heiligen".

It is established and dynamic groups that make not only the independent art scene in Linz a colourful tableau: the smart set breakfasting on the Lentos Museum's riverside terrace contribute their colours, just as the hundreds of strollers and students do who make the old town look pretty young of an evening.

A hefty dose of the wildness and avant-garde is also provided, without which urban joie-de-vivre cannot be. The Stadtwerkstatt has been open since 1979 and is the city's oldest autonomous cultural centre. In the 1980s the KAPU, which emerged from a youth organisation, started bringing punk to Linz, hardcore from Washington and hip hop from New York. At Thüsen Tak, Frank Zappa rang in modern music, as did Deep Purple co-founder Nick Simper. Apart from bands of the moment from the UK, Kurt Cobain was one of thosc who made sure Linz was always on his tour itineraries. David Bowie played here for thirty thousand fans.

In this city, the heady side of life has retained its uncompromising nature: it pushes the boat out at the Crossing Europe film festival with committed, contemporary movies. Finds electrifying common ground between pop and digitalisation at the Stream Festival. Unleashes "contemporary culture at the docks" at the Posthof and creates the freedom and spaces for what is probably Europe's biggest graffiti gallery at the Mural Harbor. Or at the Theater Phönix where classics find themselves rejuvenated and young writers on the stage. The great Linz resident Anton Bruckner said that he had achieved great things "because from my youth onward I had respect for all that is genuine and sacred". The performers, authors and directors of today's cultural scene in Linz would probably subscribe to these sentiments without reservation.

NIGHTLIFE IST HIGHLIFE

NIGHTLIFE IS HIGH LIFE

In der lauen Luft eines Sommerabends, im warmen Schein der Lichter tränkt eine heitere Intimität die Weite des Linzer Hauptplatzes. Stimmen, Düfte und Gelächter lassen hinter dem kühnen Pragmatismus das Gemüt und den Schalk dieser Stadt erahnen.

In the mild air of a summer evening, in the warm glow of the lights, the expanse of Linz main square is bathed in a cheerful intimacy. Voices, scents and laughter hint at the soul and roguish humour that this city hides behind its bold pragmatism.

Kaffeehaus
BRUCKNER

Die „Ausgeh-Meile" erstreckt sich in Linz über mehrere Meilen: von der Flanier- und Promenierzone entlang der Landstraße und des Hauptplatzes über die dicht gefüllten Schanigärten in den Gassen der Altstadt bis zur großen Kulisse auf der Donauterrasse des Lentos.

The "nightlife mile" in Linz actually covers several miles: From the promenades along Landstrasse and the main square via the crowded beer gardens in the old town lanes to the elegant location of the Lentos Museum's riverside terrace.

READ
BOOKS
BUY
BOOKS
BUY

JOSEF BAUER
Demonstration

EXPRESSIV

EXPRESSIVE

Die größte Street-Art-Galerie Europas sehen viele im Mural Harbor auf dem Linzer Hafengelände. Ursprünglich von der Stadt geduldet, später zunehmend gefördert, haben sich die Graffiti-Kunstwerke an den Mauern der Industriegebäude zu einem touristischen Magneten entwickelt.

There are many who regard the Mural Harbor at Linz docks as the biggest street art gallery in Europe. First tolerated, then increasingly promoted by the city authorities, the artworks on the walls of the industrial buildings have become a popular tourist attraction.

HUCKEY
DAN
KARL
LINZ

Zipfer
MAN
Zipfer
L 724 KE
Vale

BRAU-TRADITION

BREWING TRADITION

Gemessen und genossen am Kulturgut Bier ist Linz schon seit 1921 Kulturstadt. In der damals gegründeten „Braubank AG" wurzelt die Geschichte der heutigen Brau Union als größtes Brauereiunternehmen Österreichs. Regionale Biertraditionen pflegt das Unternehmen mit Brau-Standorten in ganz Österreich ebenso wie als Tochter des Heineken-Konzerns den Geschmack der weiten Welt.

Considering and enjoying beer as part of its culture, Linz has been a city of culture since 1921. It was then, with the foundation of the Braubank AG brewing company, that the story of Brau Union, now Austria's biggest brewery, began. The company upholds local brewing traditions with sites all over Austria, and also spreads the taste of the world at large as a subsidiary of the Heineken concern.

1
36
20 B·L·F 15
FEMINISM IS FOR EVERYBODY

BUNTE SZENE

COLOURFUL SCENE

Je später der Abend, desto lebendiger die KAPU. Das einstige Kasernengebäude aus dem 18. Jahrhundert hat eine bemerkenswerte Wandlung durchgemacht: Geführt von einem alternativen Kulturverein, treffen sich dort heute die Fans von Hip-Hop, Rock und Punk.

The later the evening, the livelier the Kapu. The former barracks from the eighteenth century have undergone a remarkable transformation: run by an alternative cultural association, fans of hip hop, rock and punk meet there today.

WIE ZU HAUSE

HOME FROM HOME

Wer das Gemütliche in seiner skurrilen Spielart liebt, fühlt sich im Thüsen Tak wie zu Hause. Bis tief in die Nacht schallt hier Hardrock in Wohnzimmer-Atmosphäre. Alles, was an den Wänden hängt und klebt, hat eine Geschichte zu erzählen. Schon Frank Zappa und Deep-Purple-Mitbegründer Nick Simper haben die Vorzüge des Hauses zu schätzen gewusst.

Lovers of cosy places with a quirky touch certainly feel at home at Thüsen Tak. Here, hard rock blares out till the small hours in a living-room atmosphere. Everything hanging or stuck on the walls has a story to tell. Frank Zappa and Deep Purple co-founder Nick Simper are among those who appreciated what the bar has to offer.

SRAM

Ronnie James Dio
KINGS OF METAL
MANOWAR
BLACK SABBATH
HEAVEN AND HELL
Thüsen Tak

Thüsen Tak
Rata Blanca
Thüsen Tak
Sommer 2020
Canary Islands
THUSENTAK INDIA

KLANG & LICHT

SOUND & LIGHT

Ein Spektakel für höchste Ansprüche bieten die Linzer Klangwolken. Eingebettet in ein Open-Air-Musikfestival, locken Laserzauber und Watt-satte Klänge jedes Jahr im Herbst um die 100.000 Besucher an die Donau und ins Stadtzentrum.

A spectacle for the most sophisticated tastes: that's the Linzer Klangwolke. Part of an open-air music festival, the laser magic and high-wattage sounds draw around a hundred thousand visitors to the Danube and the city centre in September.